YOUR BUSINESS:

MAKE IT WORK FOR *YOU*

YOUR BUSINESS: MAKE IT WORK FOR <u>YOU</u>

Ready-made Tools and
Active Spreadsheets for
Improving Performance
and Profitability

M I K E   S H A W

**KOGAN
PAGE**

YOURS TO HAVE AND TO HOLD
BUT NOT TO COPY

First published in 1997

Kogan Page Limited
120 Pentonville Road
London N1 9JN

© Mike Shaw, 1997

British Library Cataloguing in Publication Data
A CIP record for this book is available from the British Library.
ISBN 0 7494 2061 8

Typeset by Saxon Graphics Ltd, Derby
Printed in England by Clays Ltd, St Ives plc

CONTENTS

PREFACE

If you are thinking of starting a business, this isn't the book for you. If you are running a small business which cannot be improved, you don't need this book.

But if you're in business and think you could do better, read on. This book will show you the route to travel to reach your desired result – whatever that may be.

ACKNOWLEDGEMENTS

This book is based on methods developed and refined over many years in business and business counselling. It would never have seen the light of day without the help of my wife, Margaret, who kept asking, 'What does this mean?' as she typed the various drafts.

Many of the ideas in the book stemmed from a course I attended at the University of Durham Business School. I very much appreciate the help I received from Geoff Potts of that organisation.

Assistance in the design of the computing aspects came from Phil Dodd, who patiently converted me into a computer addict.

The encouragement of my friends and fellow counsellors in the Business Link movement has also been a source of strength to me in the completion of this project.

Mike Shaw
Marton, Warwickshire
April 1996

INTRODUCTION

The owners of many businesses would like to improve business performance, but seeing through the detail, the worries about paying suppliers and employees and giving the best deal to customers takes all the time they have available. They work for their businesses. This book does not tackle technical problems in your commercial field. What it does is to show you how to make your business work for *you*.

In the book you will find a set of tools. The easy way to use them is in one of the computer versions, although a manual format is provided for anyone who wants to do the calculations physically. The system of analysis, synthesis and implementation in this book has been used many times by the author to help clients. The techniques used were developed as manual techniques and only computerised later, once they were well proven.

Whichever route you follow, provided you stick to the system you will produce a practical plan to get your business working for you.

The book has two major themes: a business philosophy and a set of tools to enable you to achieve what you want from your business.

THE BUSINESS PHILOSOPHY

Owner-management is a way of life. No one can tell you as the owner-manager of your own business what you should want. This book does not attempt to prescribe ideals. The philosophy behind the book is simple. It is based on the premise that the purpose of most businesses is to provide their owners with money – money to enable the owners to do what they really want to do. This book has no part in telling you what you should want to do, only how to make the money you need.

Generally speaking, business strategies fit into three main genres: survival, long-term security and self-fulfilment. For all of these you need money. Where does that money come from? The most popular answer to that is customers, meaning sales. This leads to many wrong and harmful decisions. *The real income to any business is its gross margin* (see Chapter 3).

ABOUT THE TOOLS

The book provides you with a set of tools to improve your business. The tools are essentially to enable you to understand where your business currently stands, to analyse what you think is wrong with your business (pinpoint your dissatisfactions) and then plan your way safely to improvements.

The major tools are:

- Analysis tools
- Planning tools.

The analysis tools provided are:

- Ratio analysis form
- Market analysis form
- Organisation analysis form.

The planning tools provided are:

- The business plan
- Cashflow forecast form
- Profitability forecast form
- Project control form.

The rest of this book describes the forms and what they tell you, explains how to use these forms, and tells you what problems may be found in your business and how to use the process to solve those (and other) problems.

The book goes on to describe how to create and implement your business improvement plan. There is a worked example to show readers who feel less comfortable with balance sheets how to get from the raw data to the real information.

You don't need to read every page of the book. Each section is designed to stand alone. Experienced practitioners may prefer just to use the tools provided – in which case, that section of the book is where they should start. On the other hand, if you're not used to probing the inner workings of your business, you will find in the book the detail you need.

1

A CLOSER LOOK AT THE TOOLS

The tools provided in this book come in two principal forms: computer-based and manual. You will find the computer-based forms, which have been designed to work in most commonly found formats, on the disk which comes with the book. The manual forms (hard copy) are provided as appendices. They are:

- Ratio analysis form   Appendix 1
- Market analysis form   Appendix 2
- Organisation analysis form   Appendix 3
- The business plan   Appendix 4/4a
- Cash flow forecast form   Appendix 5
- Profitability forecast form   Appendix 6
- Project control form   Appendix 7

How to use these tools is explained in Chapter 2. These appendices appear both in the book and on the disk. Appendices 8, 9 and 10 appear in the book only. In this chapter we look at what the forms show us.

THE RATIO ANALYSIS FORM

This form (see Appendix 1) is divided into five major sections:

1. Data collection

2. Key operating ratios
3. Break-even calculations
4. Funding-need calculations
5. Banker's ratios.

If you are using the computer version, you will notice that a graph which plots sales and break-even sales is produced automatically for you. The basic format covers four years, but you can alter it to cover as many extra periods as you like just by copying the formulae across. (*Refer to your computer manual if you don't know how to do this.*)

Data collection

This section is where you enter information from your accounts. Details of how to do this are in the next chapter. If you intend to skip straight to that, please read the section on entering data, or you may create unnecessary problems for yourself.

Before entering your data, note that there are four distinct types of active cell:

1. blank
2. containing a 0
3. containing #value!
4. containing #Div/0!

If you are entering data in one of the computer-based forms, you must enter it only into the *blank* cells. The others have formulae in them which will calculate their own data from that which you enter into the blank cells. (If you enter data in those cells, you will erase the formula already in the cell.) The data collection section runs from line 7 to line 29 in the form. This is information from your accounts.

Why is the form any better than the raw accounts?

At best your raw accounts (the figures as they stand) show what you have achieved in the past, but is that good or bad? Is a profit of £1000 good? The answer is that it might be if you achieved it in a very short time using almost no resources; on the other hand, if it constituted an entire year's profit at ICI, the shareholders would not be very pleased! That is what the ratios are about. Some years ago ratio analysis acquired a bad name for itself because its pundits talked of 'ideal ratios' – by which they meant magic numbers that were said to be 'right' for a particular type of business. We aren't going to do that. What we need to do is to look at what those ratios mean for your business.

Key operating ratios

The second section of the form, from line 30 to line 44, contains the key operating ratios. If you are using the computer version, as you enter the data (lines 7–29), these ratios will be calculated automatically for you. If you are performing the task manually, you will find the formulae in Appendix 8. What do those ratios tell you? The salient points to look for are given below.

Current assets : current liabilities

To the layman the word *asset* means something good. Someone who is a real asset is hardly a millstone round your neck, but we are talking accounts here. Only an accountant could regard money owed to you as an asset. The term *current assets* really means those aspects of the business which you have to finance, but which should be converted into cash in the relatively near future. That also includes cash in hand and at the bank. (Owners of some small businesses may not understand this, but bear in mind that you haven't finished working through the book yet!)

Current liabilities represent the money you owe and can be called upon to pay in the relatively near future.

The current assets/current liabilities ratio is a critical one. It is sometimes known as *the acid test* as it is a measure of your ability to pay your way. If you are running a limited liability company, current assets must always be greater than current liabilities. If it is not, you must not take further credit and should seek immediate help from your financial adviser, your local Business Link, and/or your bank. Failure to do this can mean that the directors will lose the protection of the limited liability, and you could go to prison. It is outside the scope of this book to deal with liquidation, but please heed the warning.

If yours is not a limited liability company, you aren't obliged to follow these rules. However, a ratio of less than one, does mean you could be spending a lot of time 'robbing Peter to pay Paul' instead of getting on with the business of making money.

What should the ratio be? This is always a good question to ask, and one to which there is no right answer. The factors to consider include the nature of the asset. Is it cash or not? If it is cash, then too much of it lying around means that you aren't making efficient use of the resource. If too little, the same applies (as you waste hours dodging your creditors). Look at the way your ratios have changed over the years and try to remember which you were happier with: that's probably what's right for you. For future projects, when you are thinking of taking on that big order, just put the impact of the order into your calculation for this ratio and it will give you a good measure of how much your business will be at risk if you take it on.

Just for fun, try the same thing if your customer is a month late in paying you. It never happens, of course, but deduct from your current assets the value of your largest single debtor. That's what would happen if your biggest debtor went broke on you. Would your business be able to survive? Does this give you any ideas about what you would prefer that ratio to be, and what you need to do to achieve the level you want?

Changing the ratio can be done in four ways. To increase the ratio you can:

- increase your assets (although normally this will only be beneficial if it is the cash asset you increase);
- decrease your liabilities.

To decrease the ratio you can:

- decrease your assets (by collecting debts and taking the money out of the business to put to better use elsewhere, or reducing stocks and using the money elsewhere);
- increase your liabilities.

Sales : working capital

The value of this ratio is that it tells you how well your money is working for you. If you look at your ratio over the years you will probably see a trend. If you're in control of your finances that trend will be towards settling down at a stable level. Young businesses will not be able to see this too clearly because of the high proportion of unusual start-up demands for capital. This ratio is particularly useful when considering the big order. How much will it cost to take it on? If you operate in your normal way, you're going to need the order value multiplied by this ratio in additional working capital. Talk to your bank before you say yes: experience shows that the ratio can only get worse when you take on a bigger than normal contract – probably because you have so many other worries with the big contract that you take your eye off the financial ball. Your bank manager is more likely to have faith in your ability to manage that contract if you have talked it through with him before you say yes to the extra work. It's quite easy to find this vital information in your stuffy old accounts.

Total debt : net worth

Even if you don't appreciate the importance of this, your bank manager, or anyone else you approach for finance, will.

Why? Because it's a measure of how much of the risk you are prepared to carry yourself. Rightly or wrongly, lenders believe that if you think your idea is good you'll want as much of the proceeds for yourself as you can get. The idea of an entrepreneur sitting in his office saying to himself, 'This is too good for me to keep for myself. I must share the profits with my bank', holds little credibility with the average bank manager, who has grown cynical over years of exposure to the likes of us! During times when lending is tight, banks and other lending institutions have operated on a 1:1 ratio of debt to worth. Times are slightly easier when the market is confident, but it is still an important concept. For your own sake, it's worth bearing in mind that debt has to be paid for one way or another. If your business is steady, not suffering from seasonal or any other variations and is sure to stay that way for the duration of your debt, you can afford a higher level of debt to worth. (Please let me know what that business is!) The cost of loans must be serviced, whether you're making a profit or not.

Earnings before interest and tax : sales

I like this one. It brings home to those who want to use borrowed money just what they could have achieved with faith in themselves. Compare it to net profit/sales. How do you feel about that? You can improve the situation by borrowing less money, or by borrowing it more wisely. You can also improve it by paying less tax. Perhaps now that your accounts are starting to be more interesting, a chat to your accountant on this subject might be of value.

Net profit : sales

This is the most quoted and least understood of all the ratios. Net profit is what sole traders and partnerships pay tax on. It is also the result of the gross margin you make minus the cost of the way you legitimately decide to spend that money within your business. Even by my standards that is abstruse. If you are running a business owned by anonymous shareholders, or if your business is a publicly quoted one, of course you must pay attention to this. If you're planning to sell your business in the next four years, then you must also pay attention to it. For the rest of us it's a relatively unimportant ratio.

Net profit : net worth

In view of the comments made above with regard to net profit, you can see the importance of this ratio. It shows over the years what your trend has been, and therefore makes an assessment of the worth of your business easy to calculate from current trading figures. It also influences directly the amount of money you can borrow. This is not a ratio to run your business by, but ignore it at your peril. Too many good owner-managed businesses have been undervalued at sale time because this ratio has been deliberately depressed for tax purposes. You can never be sure when circumstances may dictate the sudden need to sell your business.

Net profit : total assets

We have already discussed the nature of assets. They are not necessarily a good thing or a bad thing, merely something the business must finance. The cost of finance per £ of asset is easy to work out for your business. Just add up all your interest and finance charges and divide them by your total asset value. If you're thinking of adding to your total assets, either by increasing current assets (stock or credit given to customers) or by buying a new fixed asset; and you don't know if it is the right thing to do from a profit point of view, this is the ratio to look at. If the increase in profit compares unfavourably with the extra finance cost, you cannot justify the asset on financial grounds.

Credit : sales

The ratios form expresses this ratio as debtors × 365/sales. The answer to this sum gives the average number of days of credit your customers take from you. You may be convinced that your customers are all good payers, so this number can sometimes come as a shock. Look at the way the ratio has varied over the past few years in your business. Are there any lessons to be learned? One common problem is that businesses always think that they have to give credit, but this is often because the company they worked for before setting up gave credit and they have just followed suit. A good general rule is that if you don't have to give credit, *don't*.

Credit leads to a potential souring of relationships between you and your customers. It can also be expensive for you, not only because of the interest you have to pay to borrow the money you are lending to your customers, but also because of the lost opportunities created by funding a shortfall because you've lent the money to your customers. It is usually easier to get money from someone who wishes to buy and who doesn't yet have the goods than from one who has had the goods and who now feels that paying you isn't particularly important.

Another area where credit causes ill-will is in the term 'net thirty days'. Most of us think we know what it means, but there are several meanings to it. It can mean that your customer pays you thirty days after the date you deliver the goods, or thirty days after he receives the invoice, or thirty days after the end of the month in which he receives the invoice . . . and so on. If you were due a critical payment and you didn't receive it when you expected to, you would feel aggrieved, and justified in chasing your customer. If within his interpretation of the rules he believed he still had several days to go, he might feel aggrieved by your pressure. The result of a favour you have done him is unhappiness for two people. One way of avoiding this problem (if you must give credit) is to mark your invoice 'payment due not later than 28/6/97' (say). There can be no doubt in this case about when payment is actually due.

Credit terms are given for a variety of reasons, some valid and some not. Valid credit would be, in my view, where a customer orders from you several times a week. In this case, bringing cash each time would be inefficient and separate cheques would play havoc with your bank charges. Summary invoicing here does make sense. Some people ask for credit because they always do, but this is not a valid reason for granting it. You don't resent the fact that you have to pay cash in your local pub, and you are happy to pay in advance for your airline ticket or a trip to the theatre. Credit control is dealt with in depth elsewhere, but here are a few useful tips.

Debts : sales

This ratio too is calculated by multiplying the heading by 365 to give the number of days' credit you are taking. In the section on credit strain we go into this in more depth. In mimicking the larger companies we are often tempted to take as much credit as we can, but why? If you have the cash, you can often get a better deal by paying at the time. The interest you will get by having the cash in the bank may not be worth the trouble and may even be totally absorbed by the cost of the stamp and the envelope when you do pay. Money you owe is the major risk to your business. As the law now stands, a debt of £750 which you cannot pay within three weeks is all that is needed for a creditor to be able to move for a winding-up order against you. This is not an experience that many enjoy.

Cost of goods sold : average stock

This ratio is sometimes referred to as stock turn, and a lot of nonsense is talked about it. At best, stock is a necessary evil. Yes, it is an asset – but we now know about assets. What is the ideal stock turn for you, is a parameter influenced by many factors such as economic order quantities, lead time on supplies, cost of storage, perishability, shrinkage, and many others. Stock control is also dealt with elsewhere, as it is a complex issue. Within the scope of this book, however, look at the way your stock turn has varied over the years. When did you feel happiest about it? Is some of your stock more productive than other items and if so, is the slower-moving stock paying for its keep by a justifiably higher gross margin? Retailers often tell me that if they do not carry enough stock on show, their customers will lack confidence in them. Fine, but have you fully explored the opportunities of having the stock on a consignment or 'sale or return' basis?

Have you any old stock – things you have had hanging about for years? If you have, it may be worth writing it off. It will reduce your profits, of course, but you pay tax on profit! Having written it off, you may either dump it if it really is unlikely to justify its storage costs or keep it if it may be saleable in the future. (Writing off means that you eliminate the asset from your books and replace it with a loss on disposal of asset. This can be offset against your tax liability.)

Fixed assets : net worth

This is a ratio frequently ignored by businesses – because it's academic, isn't it?

Well, no, it isn't. Your money has to work for you and assets are the things you must finance. If your money is tied up in fixed assets, unless those assets change in value it's doing nothing for you at all. Often I hear people say 'I can use my factory as security against a loan' and in some cases you can, but no bank would be happy with throwing you out of your factory or shop just to recover a bad loan.

Why? Because it will probably wipe you out. One of the main reasons why otherwise good businesses get into difficulties is through buying the freehold on a factory unit when times seem good. When times are bad the cash is not available for use. Cash is king: it is your ability to pay your way, not your total worth, that counts in solvency.

Is your money still working as well for you as it has in the past? This ratio will tell you.

Sales : total assets

Total assets represent everything you have to finance. This ratio tends to vary a great deal when a business is changing dramatically, and stabilises when the business is steady.

What has your ratio been doing?

What does that tell you?

If the sales/total assets ratio is falling, are you becoming complacent? If you are looking at the implication of taking on a major increase in business, how will that affect this ratio? Can you afford to fund it? If cash flow is a critical problem, does this offer you some food for thought? Would you be better off dumping some of your less well paying turnover to improve this ratio? It's useful when you are doing cash flow forecasts to check your predictions against this ratio. If the forecast shows an improvement to a level you have never achieved before, your bank manager and other potential funders are not likely to believe it!

Gross profit : sales

This is one of the most important of all the ratios, since gross profit is the measure of the real income on which your business lives. As we

21

said earlier, it pays for your expenses, enables you to prepare for the future and pays for your fun. This ratio is a measure of how hard you have to work for that income.

Look at the way the ratio has been changing. Is it better or worse? Why? Is there anything you can do to improve the situation?

By way of an apology for poor performance in this respect, I am sometimes asked, 'What can you expect in this type of business?'. That is a very good question and statistics are available from sources such as the official statistics, Kompass, your trade association, and Companies House. What do they say you can expect? What do previous years' figures show? Is there a trend? If there is a trend and it's a downward one, is it time you got into something that will pay better? All these are questions that this ratio invites you to ask. That's why it is so important!

Break-even calculations

The third section of the form (lines 45–52) is concerned with break-even calculations. Knowing what your break-even point is is of fundamental importance to business control. Let's be sure we understand what we are talking about here. Break-even occurs when gross margin equals expenses (overheads). Business people often quote break-even sales as £xxxx. Since we have travelled through the ratios together, we now understand that this is only a valid figure provided that we have achieved the target gross margin. As an example, let's consider a business where the overhead expenses are £8000 for the year. If our business is operating with a gross margin of 25 per cent, then the sales needed to give a gross margin of £8000 are four times £8000 – and that is £32000. It would be correct for our business owner to say that his break-even on these sales was a turnover of £32000. The same business operating at a gross margin of ten per cent, however, is a very different case. At 10 per cent margin we need to sell £10 of turnover to create £1 of gross margin. For the same £8000 of overhead our break-even sales now become £80000. If you forget this, you could be chasing sales and making yourself worse off. Chasing sales usually means giving some reduction in price, and that usually means a reduction in gross margin.

Giving credit will usually mean a drastic worsening of your cash flow position.

The break-even gap

This is the difference between your break-even sales and your actual sales. It is extremely important because it is on this figure that you make your profit. If you look at the graph at the bottom of your worksheet (for those working with the computer version), or if you create the graph by plotting break-even sales and actual sales for each year in your study, what does it tell you? Is there a trend? Is that trend favourable? It may help your analysis if you write on the graph the point where significant changes occurred. Things like 'bought new XYZ machine'; 'took on ABC contract'; 'employed/sacked Fred'. Does your decision appear to be vindicated? What do you need to do to get it right? For many businesses the picture this graph produces gives a startling insight into what the business is about. Think about what it tells you. If you feel there is a message trying to get out but you can't identify it, try getting help. Your local Business Link, your accountant or your banker will find the document you have produced an excellent starting point for a productive session with you.

Quick profit

This is produced by multiplying the break-even gap by the profit margin/sales ratio. It should be very nearly equal to your net profit figure in line 16 of the spreadsheet. If it's not, something odd – or something of a non-trading nature – has influenced the profit figure in your accounts. The quick profit figure is the more reliable indicator of your trading profit. How do you feel about the result?

Quick profit/sales

See the comments made on net profit/sales ratio.

Funding-need calculations

The first eleven items of this section are repeated from elsewhere in the spreadsheet and are just grouped here for convenience, so that you can see at a glance where your hard-won funding gets used. As with all of the ratios, it's not so much the value of any one figure that is important but the changes year by year and how you feel about them. The two lines covering net working capital and its percentage to sales have traditionally been used by people who understand about money as a guide to how much it would cost you in extra finance required to take on that juicy big new order you've been offered. Indeed, in the absence of anything better it is a good quick guide and has already been discussed (see sales : working capital). The concept introduced here of creditor strain and true working assets are, I feel, more appropriate in modern times when the fear of a debtor (someone who owes money) becoming insolvent is a major worry to businesses. This fear sometimes causes people to take panic action against otherwise stable businesses who may be dealing with a company rumoured to be unable to pay its bills. What, then, is creditor strain?

Creditor strain

Creditor strain is the extra credit which a business takes without authorisation. This could be trade credit strain (ie not paying your suppliers on time) or preferential creditor strain (an unauthorised overdraft, or being late paying your taxes). It is a way of life for some businesses, but is very dangerous – particularly if you keep in mind the earlier comments on insolvency. It is in any case funding which you may be using in your business, and you need to take it into consideration when you look at the ratios relating to working capital. You may have to find some or all of your credit strain finance very quickly if rumours start about your solvency. Persistent use of this type of finance may lead to withdrawal of your credit facilities.

The figure used in the trade creditor calculation is based on 10 per cent permissible credit. If your permitted credit is more than, or less than that, you will need to edit the formula in the formula bar for this. Preferential credit is based on a 5 per cent figure. Both these figures are in line with most common practice today.

True net working assets

The significance of this figure is in its use as a ratio against sales. If you are planning an expansion, the working assets you'll need to finance it (or working capital) will be this ratio times the new turnover figure. You will need to make sure in advance that the finance is available or you'll fall into the trap of over-trading (see Chapter 3).

Banker's ratios

The sixth section of the form, headed banker's ratios, has been included for the benefit of those who are going to present the results of their analysis and their plan to their bank. Bankers use these additional ratios to help them to see just how safe a loan prospect you are.

It might equally be argued that if you are proposing to use your own money in a business scheme, you would want to know how 'fragile' your plan is, even though you feel you have erred on the safe side.

The banker's ratios are summarised below.

Profit sensitivity

This is a measurement of the likelihood of your failing to reach your profit margin. In this ratio we look at the break-even gap as a percentage of total sales. Clearly if you can break even at 10 units and you are predicting sales of 100, you are fairly safe! Even a sales disaster resulting in only 50 per cent of target means you will still make a profit from your break-even gap of 40 units (50 – 10). If, on the other hand, you were expecting to make the same profit off 100 units, but your break-even sales were, say, 95 units, then the sales disaster of 50 units would leave you with a loss. The situations in which this latter case would apply are in operations with relatively high fixed cost and also in the start-up of new operations and processes in which the output is well below the design potential for the plant and the market.

Capital gearing

Gearing is always a sensitive issue, with different authorities giving differing advice. It is the ratio between:

$$\frac{\text{Borrowings}}{\text{Shareholders' funds (owner's funds)}}$$

At the moment, banks are fairly cautious and like to see 1:1 as a working norm. They defend this along the lines of 'You take half the risk and the bank takes half, so that's fair.'

The factors which need to be considered are:

- How stable is the profit month by month? Interest has to be paid whether or not you make profit.
- How do you feel about debt? Some adjust more readily than others to the responsibility.

- How hard do you want you money to work for you? The harder it works, the more (proportionally to your borrowing) the potential returns for each pound of your capital – but also the greater the risk (see example at Figure 1.1).

Case	Total working capital	Borrow-ings	Profit (Loss)		Interest paid*	Return on your capital	
	£	£	£	%	£	£	%
1	100 000	50 000	20 000	20	5000	15 000	30
2	100 000	50 000	10 000	10	5000	5000	10
3	100 000	50 000	0	0	5000	−5000	−10
4	100 000	50 000	−10 000	−10	5000	−15 000	−30
5	100 000	10 000	20 000	20	1000	19 000	21
6	100 000	10 000	10 000	10	1000	9000	10
7	100 000	10 000	0	0	1000	−1000	−1.1
8	100 000	10 000	−10 000	−10	1000	−11 000	−12
9	100 000	90 000	20 000	20	9000	11 000	110
10	100 000	90 000	10 000	10	9000	1000	10
11	100 000	90 000	0	0	9000	−9000	−90
12	100 000	90 000	−10 000	−10	9000	−19 000	−190

*Interest at 10 per cent assumed throughout

Figure 1.1 *Risk demonstration model*

In Figure 1.1 you can see how the gearing works. In each case, the working capital remains the same. In cases 1–4 it has been assumed that half of that has been raised by borrowing at 10 per cent per annum. You can see that with good profits (20 per cent):

		Return
at gearing	1:10 (10%)	21%
	1:1 (50%)	30%
	9:10 (90%)	110%

So with good profits, high gearing gives you a very much better return on your money. However, if you look at the 90 per cent gearing (cases 9–12), you can see that if the profit is less than £9000 (9 per cent), you would get no return at all from your investment. At a 10 per cent loss you would lose almost double your money.

Banks are well aware of this. They are also aware of the temptation on the part of the borrower in such a situation to cut his losses. You can therefore understand why they like to be sure you have sufficient equity to stay hooked.

You have perhaps noticed where you and the bank take what they say is equal risk, 1:1. In the example shown, if you make 12 per cent profit, both you and the bank make 10 per cent return on your cash. If you look at what happens to a 10 per cent loss, the bank makes 10 per cent profit and you make 30 per cent loss.

You don't need to be very sophisticated at finance to look at the impact of that 30 per cent loss on the asset base to see whether a borrower can afford both in good and fair circumstances to borrow the sum mentioned. An assessment of the likelihood of failure to reach profit has already been discussed under profit sensitivity.

Interest cover

The final 'banker's ratio' covered here is interest cover. This is a measure that banks use to give comfort to themselves. The way it is worked out is:

$$\frac{\text{EBIT (earnings before interest and tax)}}{\text{interest costs}}$$

Banks usually prefer to see a ratio of approximately 3:1 for this, based on the assumption of one-third each for interest, tax and dividends (ie your return).

This may give you no joy at all, but now you know how they think. Chapter 2 will tell you about how to use this information.

The final section of the ratio analysis form is the graph which plots two lines for each year entered: sales and break-even sales. If you have used the computer-based model, this will be plotted for you. If not, plot the values in line 11 and 47 – preferably in different colours – in the space provided.

The use of this graph is explained in Chapter 2. Many clients looking at this graph have been able to put their finger straight onto the problem which has been worrying them for ages: in many cases they have also been able to see the solution to those problems.

MARKET ANALYSIS FORM

Appendix 2 contains the market analysis form which is useful as an aid to strategic planning. It is also useful as a device to enable you to evaluate your past performance in the market place. Looking backward – where have you come from in terms of customer and products (in the same period covered by the accounts entered into the ratio analysis).

Where do you intend to go?

How to use this form is discussed in Chapter 2.

ORGANISATION ANALYSIS FORM

Appendix 3 is the organisation analysis form. It is divided vertically into three main sections: marketing, resources and management. There are many ways in which these aspects of your business can be represented, but many people find that this form helps to highlight what the proposed changes will do to their business.

Chapter 2 describes how to use the form. The left-hand sector of the form is intended as a 'tick box' sector, the right-hand one so that you can see at a glance how much it will cost and how long it will take to implement the changes you are planning.

BUSINESS PLAN

Appendices 4 and 4a are business plan formats. Some business owners believe that they only need a business plan when they want to borrow money from the bank or other lending institution. Why? The fact that the bank needs to see a plan should at least provoke the question 'What for?'

The business plan is merely a statement in advance of what you expect to achieve in your business within a given time limit, and how you intend to go about it. The two words 'expect' and 'intend' are deliberate. You cannot know what the final results will be, but you do need something to aim at or otherwise knowing where to go next is extremely difficult (as is recognising when you've got there).

The two formats are based closely on those used by Business Link Leicestershire, but they share their features with many others. Regularly occurring contents are outlined below.

Business aims and objectives

This is a statement of what the business is about and where you are trying to go with it. The mechanism for filling in the plan is described in the next chapter. For the owner-manager whose business is also a way of life, this is the section in which you think clearly about what you want out of life, and consequently from your business.

If you seriously want your business to work for you, then this is where it starts to do so. The more clear you are about your objectives, the easier the rest will become. For instance, if your objective is to get rich, the market research programme could be extremely complex, because you will have ruled out nothing. Being more precise helps with the measurement process.

The business plan goes on to outline the markets, resources and management needed in the business (this links to the organisation analysis form). A section is also provided for 'risk management' and financial aspects.

CASH FLOW FORECAST

Appendix 5 is a format for a cash flow forecast. If you are working on the computer-based model, you need only enter numbers appropriate to your business. As you do that, the totals (cells which contain 0 in the draft) will be calculated for you automatically. Data entered in and below line 7 marked 'cash sales' is in active cells (cells to which control formulae apply).

When you have entered all the data (and, if appropriate, worked out the totals), looking at the bottom line will show you if you have adequate funds to do what you plan to do. This is probably the most important document you will produce: as we said earlier, businesses do not fail because they do not make profit; they fail because they run out of cash.

You should enter money coming into and going out of the business in the month in which you can realistically expect the transaction to take place. For instance, if you sell £1000 of goods in January with credit to get paid in July, then on the cash flow form put the £1000 in July *not* in January.

PROFITABILITY FORECAST

Appendix 6 contains the profitability forecast. Many people new to business planning (and even some who are not so new to it) have difficulty understanding the difference between this and the cash flow forecast – especially as the forms look so similar.

Here is an example to illustrate the difference. I buy a box of pens from my wholesaler for £10 and sell them on 30 days credit to my customer for £30. The share of expenses they must carry is £10 per month. Therefore, from a profitability point of view, at the end of the month I have this:

Sales £30
Cost of sales £10
Gross margin £20
Expenses £10
Net profit £10

From a cash flow point of view, I have spent £10 on the pens, plus £10 on expenses, so I am £20 out of pocket.

In essence the cash flow tells you how much money you need to obtain. The profitability forecast shows whether or not you can afford to pay for that money out of the business. The other major difference between cash flow and profitability is the way in which we enter data. For example, when you go to tax your car you pay the road fund licence fee for the period (12 months or whatever). In cash flow terms we show the whole amount paid out in the month when we paid it. In our profitability forecast we must divide that amount by 12 and allocate it to each month since the expense has been incurred for the whole period.

The way in which the form is laid out is consistent with the way in which taxation matters are dealt with. Generally speaking, the 'direct costs' vary with sales, whereas the 'expenditure' or overheads remain unchanged for the most part independent of sales. This makes looking at your 'fixed costs' very simple.

PROJECT CONTROL FORM

Appendix 7 is your project control form. In order to achieve the improvements you have built into your plan, you will have isolated a number of things you must do, or projects, such as *Produce new marketing leaflet* or *Sack Fred*. This form is intended at the analysis and planning stage to be the paper on which you record the changes you intend to make and the length of time you have given yourself to do them in. It is intended to be used as a Gantt chart. Assume that the two projects *marketing leaflet* and *Fred* are independent and are going to take place in months 3 and 4 respectively (see Figure 1.2).

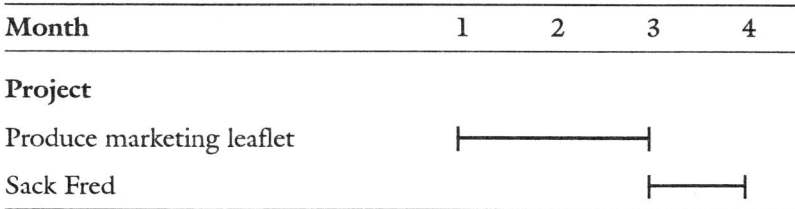

Month	1	2	3	4
Project				
Produce marketing leaflet		⊢————————⊣		
Sack Fred			⊢————⊣	

Figure 1.2   *Gantt chart — coincident but independent activities*

Let us say that the marketing brochure – allowing for writing, photography, design and printing – will take two months. If it is to be ready in month 3, we must start it at the beginning of month 1. The vertical lines show the start and finish of each project.

In the same situation, let us assume that sacking Fred is in some way related to getting the brochures out and we want to be certain they are in our hands well before we sack him. We now show the same information as:

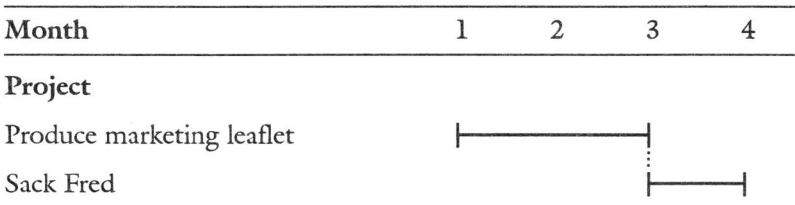

Month	1	2	3	4
Project				
Produce marketing leaflet		⊢————————⊣		
Sack Fred			⊢————⊣	

Figure 1.3   *Gantt chart — related dependent activities*

Fred goes at the same time, but the dotted line shows the relationship between the two events.

31

2

USING THE TOOLS

In this chapter you will find the 'how to' information. There are two sections – one for those using the manual version and one for computer-based versions. Most of you will probably be using an up-to-date Windows-based PC with a spreadsheet package such as Excel 5, which is what our spreadsheets were produced with.

To make your business work well for you, you will need to go through the following steps:

1. Analyse
2. Identify areas of dissatisfaction
3. Identify possible solutions
4. Evaluate solutions
5. Decide on action to take
6. Create your plan – with targets (dates and values)
7. Implement your plan
8. Monitor your plan, ensuring that you achieve your targets.

In Chapter 1 we listed the three analysis tools: ratio analysis form, marketing analysis form and organisation analysis form.

RATIO ANALYSIS FORM

The floppy disk which comes with this book includes a file called *ratan*. This is an Excel 5 file, so open it as such from your computer, and immediately save it onto your hard disk under a different name. (I use my client's company name or short form, plus an 'r' for *ratan* and a number to show which version of the spreadsheet this is). It is important to choose a distinguishing system for your file names as this one will be the first in a series, and later on you will need to be able to tell which is which.

Saving to a different file name leaves you with an untouched original file, and you won't run the risk of deleting vital formulae by mistake.

It is important to use the most up-to-date information available, so contact your accountant if you are waiting for a set of accounts.

Your screen should show a document which looks like Appendix 1. If it doesn't look like that, you may need to seek advice by writing, e-mailing or phoning the *Your business: make it work for you* help desk*.

From your accounts, enter in the boxes marked 1st, 2nd, 3rd and 4th the years you are going to cover in your analysis. If the latest data you have available is for 1995, for instance, then put 1995 as 4th, 1994 as 3rd and so on. If you are missing one year's data (in this example, let's say 1993 is missing) leave the box for 2nd blank and enter 1992 into the box marked 1st. Later on you'll see how to deal with this type of situation.

Enter your data year by year from your accounts into the *blank* lines 8–28.

Lines 12, 15, 21, 22 and 23 have formulae in them. Don't enter data in these. If you are reading this after putting something into one of those boxes, don't panic. Just go back to it and hit SPACEBAR or DELETE – this will empty the cell. If you are using Excel 5, move to the next 'unadulterated' cell on the same line (either right or left will do), then position your mouse pointer on the bottom right corner so that it changes from an arrow head into a black cross: +. With the mouse in that position, press the normal mouse button and drag across to the 'adulterated' cell. When that square shows as highlight-ed, the formula will have been restored, so now release the mouse but-ton. Any problems doing this, seek help!

!

You will find it easier to enter all the data for one year at a time. The convention with accounts is to show two years on the same page for comparison purposes. Remember that the latest year's figures are usu-ally in the left-hand column.

E-mail: mike@mshaw.demon.co.uk
Telephone: 01643 707883
Address: Glenmore Lodge, 24 Glenmore Road, Minehead, TA24 5BH

Another convention, when plotting graphs, is to have the oldest data on the left and the newest on the right. Again, to avoid the problems caused by cross-over data, it is best to deal with one year at a time. It takes only a few moments longer and can save you hours of frustration sorting out mistakes.

If you have any doubts about how to enter the data from your accounts, look first at Appendix 9. This shows a complete worked example, accompanied by discussions about why you need to enter the data in a particular way.

There are two key reasons for doing this analysis, one associated with improving your business and gaining from it what you want, and the other concerned with raising money from lenders or through venture capitalists. The more sophisticated lenders will themselves use a version of this form.

Once you have entered all the data for your most recent financial year, do the same for the preceding three years. It is important to be consistent about this. If you have changed accountant during this period, you may find changes in convention. Sometimes the difference in approach can involve quite disturbing changes in convention – such as moving labour costs in a manufacturing business from direct costs into expenses. . . .

If you look at your accounts (and your profitability forecast), you will see that labour appears as a direct cost and 'employee wages' as an expense. It is more important here to be consistent through the four years so that you compare like with like than it is to be correct.

Having entered all the data, save your file and print out a copy. You will have two pages of printout, as in Appendix 1.

One school of thought, and an acceptable management philosophy, maintains that the ratios have meaning in themselves and can be prescribed as ideals. I do not believe that there is such a thing as an ideal ratio: your business is different from every other business, isn't it? The banker may have little else to guide him about yours, though, and so he can be forgiven for using the ratios this way. In Chapter 1 (under banker's ratios) you have already seen that bankers like to see interest cover at 3:1. This is a prime example of a prescribed ratio.   .

To help them assess your business, bankers also often use *industrial averages* data, which you can get from *Key Industrial Ratios,* published by Dun & Bradstreet International. Your local library may be able to obtain this for you, or you may find a copy at your local Business Link; alternatively, contact the *Your business: make it work for you* help desk (see page 33 for details).

You can assess your business in a similar way if you want to, but unless you are seeking financial support, I don't recommend it. Knowing what goes on in your industry and why your company is or is not average is useful, but it does not make sense to change the way in which you operate just because you differ from the industry norm.

Business analysts used to make the comparison between Ford and General Motors – a relevant insight into the dangers of industry norms. Both Ford and General Motors manufactured motor cars. In the 1960s Ford bought raw materials such as iron ore and used its own steel-making plants, foundries and so on to make a high proportion of its vehicles from basic materials. General Motors, on the other hand, bought in most of its components from other manufacturers and assembled them into finished vehicles. In consequence, the two companies' operations were totally different from one another, and so would their ratios be. Treat industry norms with care.

What you can rely on with the ratios is your own company's performance. If you have been consistent about entering the data, the ratios will be valid for you.

Look at each ratio in turn, noting any significant changes from year to year. Put a mark against the ones that worry you. If you are not sure of the significance of a ratio look back at Chapter 1 and read the section which relates to that ratio. Look again at the sections you have marked and see if there are any messages there for you. Look at the graph on page 2 of your printout. How do you feel about that? In Chapter 3 we look at common business problems. Why not look at that now if you are not yet sure what you should be worrying about (or what to worry about most) here? Remember that you started this exercise because you weren't happy with some aspect of your business. Does it show up in your analysis?

When you have identified to your own satisfaction the items you want to change, make a list of them and ask yourself whether those changes require the cooperation of your existing customers or the acquisition of new customers? If either is the case, take your first look at the market analysis form. If the answer to the question is *no*, then you can progress directly to the organisation analysis form.

MARKET ANALYSIS FORM

This form (Appendix 2) is a simple matrix with products on one axis and customer types on the other.

As you are at the analysis stage, you have said what you think is wrong with your business and you feel that doing something about it will have some impact on your market. All you need·to do at the moment is to mark the square in the matrix where the main effect of your proposed changes will be felt. To help you do that, read the content of the cells in Figure 2.1 and mark your chart by putting a cross in the appropriate cell. You may of course mark more than one square if you are going to change some of your products or services but not others.

Product/Market	Same customers	More of the same type of customer	Totally new type of customer
The same product(s)	1 If your plan envisages no change in products or customers, mark here and proceed to the internal factors section in the organisation analysis form.	2 If you are sticking to the same product but need more customers like the best ones you already have, state what type and how many more you need.	3 If you are sticking to the same product, but intend to tackle a whole new market, state what type and how many of those customers you need.
Modified product(s)	4 What modifications will you make? Have you talked to your most trusted customers about it? What impact will this have on the business?	5 What modifications will you make? Have you talked to your most trusted customers about it? What impact will this have on the business? How many new customers will you need?	6 What modifications will you make? Have you talked to your most trusted customers about it? What impact will this have on the business? What type and how many new customers will you need?
New product(s)	7 What is the new product? Have you talked to your most trusted customers about it? What impact will this have on the business?	8 What is the new product? Have you talked to your most trusted customers about it? What impact will this have on the business? How many new customers will you need?	9 What is the new product? Have you talked to your most trusted customers about it? What impact will this have on the business? What type and how many new customers will you need?

Figure 2.1 *Market analysis form*

Going on to the second stage of quantifying the change is something you will be doing later. It is enough at this point to identify the main areas of change.

Compare where you have put your cross on your market analysis form with the comments in Figure 2.1. Does the result of your comparison suggest any dangers?

This is a useful form for risk evaluation, both at this stage and when evaluating solutions later. Look where you have marked your cross. If the changes you intend to make have no impact on your market, you would have marked square 1: this is where the least risk lies, since you know both the products and the customers.

The next position of least extra risk is square 2, as you are still providing the same products and/or services to the same types of business. You are less likely to come unstuck because of a new problem. You will note that I have not said you can use the same sales technique since, although the new customers will be using your products/services in the same way as your old customers, the benefit that each customer derives from your product is unique to that customer. Effective selling aims at just that special difference.

In square 3 the risk is greater than in square 2 because, while you are selling the same product/service as before, it is to different types of customers. For example, a window cleaner still cleans windows, but instead of just doing so at more houses (square 2), he decides to target shop and/or office windows (square 3).

The risks are clearly different – not getting large windows 'smear free' might well annoy a shopkeeper but go unnoticed in the home. Falling from the 12th floor, which is not unlikely when cleaning windows at some offices, is most unlikely to happen to the window cleaner of domestic properties.

The risks associated with a move into square 4 should not be underestimated. It is the same customers who are at the moment loyal, but offering a modified product or service which goes wrong would enable the competition to move in and take your traditional business from you. Change to the new is not always a success.

Moving to square 7, especially if the new product is a substitution rather than an addition, is still more risky. Even with additional new products or services, the comments appropriate to square 4 are particularly applicable here.

The two routes described above are far less risky than the route through 1–5–9, which involves not only changing the entire basis on which you are doing business but also has a far greater chance of failure.

ORGANISATION ANALYSIS FORM

The organisation analysis form in Appendix 3 is the next of the analysis tools. You can see that it is divided vertically into three main sections and also into three horizontally.

At the analysis stage you are only concerned with the first four columns (ie Section 1), which need to be marked to show what impact your proposed changes will have. The 'existing' column is there so that you can confirm to yourself 'I do not mean to make any changes in this area'.

The 'extension to existing' column should be marked for 'more of the same'. 'Modified' and 'entirely new' are self-explanatory.

Some useful tips at this stage include taking each section of the form in isolation, ie marketing, resources and management.

Marketing

When looking at marketing, you have already used the market analysis form, but it is worth using this exercise to ask yourself a few more questions.

Customer needs

1. Do you know who your key customers are?
   - What do your key customers have in common?
   - How does this set them apart (a) from other customers and (b) from non-customers?
   - Does this suggest anything to you?
2. Do you know what your key customers need/want from you? (Have you asked them or are you guessing?)
3. How does your range of products and/or services meet that need?
4. How is your range of products different in this respect from that of your competition?

Market performance

How well are you doing in your market?

1. Look at your key ratios for the past two or three years, checking for changes in any of these areas:
   - Profit/sales (see ratio analysis form)
   - Profit/sales for each product (service) group (Do you have enough information in your systems to tell you this?)
   - Profit/sales for each geographical area.
2. List your customers by order of sales value:
   - Does the 80/20 rule apply (80 per cent of sales coming from 20 per cent of customers; 80 per cent of profit coming from 20 per cent of customers)?
   - Are they the same 20 per cent in both cases?
   - Does this tell you anything?

Competition awareness

1. List your main competitors.
2. What are the main strengths and weakness of each of them?
3. What changes have there been in your market place over the last three years?
4. What changes do you expect to take place during the coming year?
5. What mechanisms do you have to ensure that you monitor what is going on in your market?
6. Do you allocate some time each month to make sure you know what is going on in the market? (Sources include trade associations, national and trade press, market research.)

Selling

1. Who does the selling in your business?
2. Do they know the benefits (unique selling points) of your products (services)?
3. If you are the main sales person and do most of the work yourself, or if you have a sales force working for you, have you allocated enough resource on a *regular and planned* basis to ensure that your sales targets are met?

4. Do you set sales targets?
5. Do you meet your targets regularly?
6. If you have decided that increased income for your business is essential, will this be through (a) more customers or (b) better returns from existing customers?
7. If you need more customers, how many more customers do you need?
8. Have you allocated enough resource of whatever type for this?
9. Does what your customer really wants get communicated to you?
10. How is that information used to determine your approach to the customer?
11. What is your sales conversion rate? Are you satisfied with it?

Marketing mix

1. What is your pricing policy? Why?
2. Is it the only policy appropriate in your market? Is it the best possible policy for you?
3. How does your message reach the customer – advertising, personal recommendation, etc? Is that effective?
4. What do you do actively to promote sales? Is that enough?
5. Do you give after-sales service? How do you rate your performance in this respect?
6. Do you take the opportunity to use PR for your business, letting your customers (or the press) know when you have something worth while to say?
7. Do you present your product/service well? Little things make all the difference – have you looked into these? What do your customers think? A good example here is the gardening services contractor who has a written statement of scope of work for his clients. The document is neatly typed and looks businesslike. It has won him business where other similar suppliers were regarded as cowboys.
8. Do you use sponsorship – either to get support for yourself or to provide it for others? If so, do you (or your sponsors) receive value for money?

With the answers to these questions, you should now be in a position to tackle the marketing section, in order to bring about the results you have said you want to achieve. Mark the form accordingly with a cross in the appropriate column. Mark all items for the sake of completeness; eg if there is no change planned put your cross in the 'existing' column.

Resources

Finance is deliberately omitted from the resources, since this is an issue strongly influenced by what you want to do (this will appear when we develop the alternatives) and what you feel comfortable with.

Thinking of the changes you have identified, write down how you think making those changes will affect the resources you will need.

Management

Assessing management is easier in a situation of 'them and us' but when 'them' is 'us' it is harder to be objective. Thinking about the following questions may help.

Production

This covers both the making of goods and the provision of services.

Utilisation
1. How well do you use:
   (a) labour? (b) equipment? (c) space?
   Have you any records to support your assessment?
2. Does the 'labour' element consist solely of your efforts or that of others as well? Do you waste other people's time by doing their job for them?
3. Is equipment well used, or are you either using labour to do a task which could easily be mechanised or do you hoard equipment as a hobby?
4. Is space well utilised? Look at your work space. What do you think a customer or an outsider would see? Why not ask? Does the answer tell you anything?

Efficiency
1. Are the above resources used efficiently? Or do you use time, space or equipment wastefully?
2. Do you have any measure or record of this?

41

Quality
1. The positive side of quality is happy customers? What percentage of your customers tell you your products/services are good?
2. Do you enjoy a good reputation for quality? Do you know how much you scrap in order to keep that reputation?
3. Do you know how much rework goes into keeping that reputation?
4. What does that reworking cost you?
5. Is there anything you can do to reduce that cost without losing the reputation for quality that you *need*?
6. Do you have a system for dealing effectively with customer complaints?
7. Have you lost any customers as a consequence of quality issues?
8. If you look at what you spend in order to get new customers, advertising, quoting, promoting, selling etc, and divide the annual cost by the number of new customers less the number of customers lost, you arrive at the cost of quality.

Example

Cost of sales and promotion	£5000
Number of customers	35
New customers this year	10
Old customers lost this year	8

Cost of losing a customer

$$= \frac{5000}{(10-8)} = \text{£2500}$$

What did poor quality cost you?

9. Have you thought of implementing a proper system to reduce that cost?

Wastage
1. There are lots of ways of measuring wastage, many peculiar to the type of business. Do you have a system to tell you what wastage your business has?

2. What would be the most effective measure of wastage for you?
3. What does this tell you?

Markets
1. Having answered the marketing section in detail, are you managing this well?
2. Do you have the resources, systems and information to ensure that you do achieve your goals in this area?

Finance
Businesses do not fail because they don't make enough profit. They fail because they run out of cash. Since the real income of your business is gross margin, do you have the necessary information and, if so, do you use that information to control your business?

Run a health check on your financial systems and then tick the organisation form according to the changes you mean to make. You have marked up the ratios you intend to change. Are the major changes you contemplate to do with cash, or are they profit-related?

Cash management

This needs only a few simple controls for most small businesses. Cash management is about getting the money in which you are owed, and paying out the money you owe in a sensible way.

1. Do you know how much money you are owed?
2. Do you know who owes you the money which is overdue?
3. Do you know by how much it is overdue?
4. Do you have a system for monitoring it?
5. Do you know how much you will have to pay out this month and next month?
6. Will you have enough cash to meet these bills?

Profit management

1. Are you charging enough?
2. What would happen if you increased your prices?
3. Do you have an information system to tell you this?

> Paul, whose business used the analysis system outlined in this book, had been thinking of putting up prices as margins were poor. Competition was fierce, however, so he decided not to take action because of losing turnover. He calculated that the turnover he would lose would be equivalent to the output of one of his retail centres. The cost savings on overhead, plus the additional margin on the remaining sales, gave him higher profits.

4. Does your financial system allow you to see at a glance what your products or services in each sale have really cost you?
5. What about those costs? Is there a way in which you can deal with your suppliers to reduce the cost of what you buy? This does not necessarily mean driving a harder bargain. You may be paying for something you don't want and its provision may well be something your supplier finds a problem to deliver. You won't know if you don't ask!
6. Are you paying too much for labour? You don't have to be the meanest payer in the district to score in this area. You just have to be the best at getting value for money from what you do pay for.
7. What about overheads? Do they really make sense? Many small businesses wind up with overhead expenses because they want a particular 'item'. (For example one of my clients is in love with tools. He buys them as a hobby. He knows the business does not justify the purchases, but he buys the tools anyway because he enjoys them. That's fine. What you need to look at here is all the overhead expenditure, to see if it is all earning its keep. . . .
8. It is also worth reflecting on the amount of effort you had to put into finding out this information and whether a change to your finance system is indicated.

Technical issues

This area is often the one business people think of first when examining their business.

1. Is your technology making the best use of your time?
2. Are you making the best use of your technology? It is all very well to have the latest computer, for instance, but have you been properly trained to use it?
3. When all else fails, do you read the instruction book?

DEVELOPING SOLUTIONS

Using the analysis tools, you have now identified the major areas of dissatisfaction. If you are satisfied that you have identified enough for now, you may proceed to the stage of developing solutions. If you are not happy that you have got to the bottom of things, you may wish to read the next chapter before going further.

I have named the symptoms of the most common business ailments, and these may help with the analysis of your own business.

Whichever of these two routes you have taken, you are now ready to take your list of 'ills' and targets and put them together as an improvement plan. Begin by writing your list down. Do this in a random fashion, not keeping to the lines, but making sure that all the items to be changed are on a single side of the paper. Now look for unifying threads so that you can combine genuinely related issues into a single project.

Jim's list of problems looked like this:

- Sales behind target
- Quality poor
- Returns from customers high
- Margins low
- No quality system.

These items were scattered across the page when Jim did this exercise, as he was too involved in the day-to-day 'firefighting' to notice them. He had only included 'quality system' because some of his customers were making noises about BS5750 (ISO9000). Watching the look of astonishment and delight on his face as he linked these items together was worth far more than the fee he was paying for my advice!

By combining the different 'threads' you can rationalise the confusing array of problems into a few logically based projects. The number of projects you can take on at any one time will depend on the size of your business. Appendix 10 contains the project assessment form which is sometimes useful in helping you to prioritise your projects. Alternatively, you may prefer to work straight onto the project control form in Appendix 7.

To record impact of change, take each change item and give it a number. Then think about what that change means in terms of each activity area on the form in Appendix 10 and enter the number in the appropriate column. When prioritising, use two classifications: 'Urgent' and 'Important'. Allocate priorities 'U1', 'U2,' . . . 'I1', 'I2' and so on.

When deciding the improvement plan sequences, take account of these factors but at the same time make sure that logic is followed. It usually isn't wise to build the roof before the foundations, but sometimes amazing advantages can be achieved by doing just that. Look at the changes you need to make, and record them on your project improvement plan in the order of overall priority. Using the form as a bar chart you can now draw in lines representing project durations. If one project needs to be completed before another can start, link them on your chart. When you've made the assessments of need, enter the cost of achieving this into the column in the form in Appendix 10 and/or Appendix 3. You are now in a position to look at the cash flow forecast.

The 'first run' cash flow forecast is an extremely handy tool at this stage. You know what you want to do, but does it make financial sense and *can you afford to do it*?

What I suggest you do is to take the improvement projects you have just identified and list them on the project control form. Most business people will be familiar with this kind of planning too (Gantt chart – see Chapter 1). Note that, at this stage, you have *identified* the things you would like to do, and now you are looking at the practicality of applying those solutions. In other words, you are *evaluating*. At this stage, the work can still be in draft form and include best guess information. If you are not completely happy with the quality of the data you have, make a note of the assumptions you are making based on that data. If the success of the project (or your business) really hinges on a specific piece of information, it makes sense to get it right, even if it costs a few pounds to do so.

Cash flow forecast

Now that you have entered the project detail on the draft project control form, you can move on to do your cash flow forecast. At this stage you can choose between two ways of going about your cash flow forecast.

One way is to group overheads together and put the annual sum divided by 12 for each month. Next, add a line for direct costs (labour and materials), a line for project costs (as and when they occur) and modify the sales line to take account of the changes you expect will result from your efforts.

The alternative is to put in the itemised costs as and when they fall due – ie, doing it properly. The method you choose may depend on whether outsiders (bank or other lender) will be involved. If you are going to have to show the plan to others, you may as well fill in the expense detail accurately. If you are working on the computer version of this system, copying across accurate data from one trial scheme to another takes no more time than copying approximate data.

On the floppy disk, find a spreadsheet entitled APP05.XLT. Open this and save it immediately as Sheet 1 or whatever title you prefer. You don't have any calculations to do if you're using the computerised form. If you're doing the job manually, you'll need the form included as Appendix 5.

It doesn't matter where you start: the major problem for most people is actually getting started. You'll find it easier to put in the definite things first, so if the rent is £400 a month and not expected to change during the year, put that in. Once you make a start on putting things in, the job gets easier.

To start with, put costs in when you would expect to meet them. For instance, if you are going to produce a sales brochure and you want it in three months' time, look at your improvements chart to find what you think it would cost and enter that figure in the month you will have to pay the bills in order to get your brochure when you want it to be ready. Work on this principle with all the numbers.

Above the main document you will see a line for order intake. If you give credit to your customers, use this line to enter when you take the orders, and the sales lines to indicate when you will get the money. Don't forget to enter the opening bank balance at the start of the sheet. If changes are likely to be the result of your improvement projects, take into account the phasing of those projects, so keep your plan by you when doing this exercise.

Be as realistic as you can – neither too pessimistic nor over-optimistic. When you have completed entering your data, look at the bottom line. Does it show a realistic scenario? If it shows substantial negative balances, would your bank be willing to entertain that? Is the position really what you want?

If you have produced a plan you are happy with, then you're ready to start making it happen; if you are still not comfortable about it, you can move things around within the plan to suit yourself. If you're using the computer model, what I recommend is that you save your new sheet as Sheet 1, and then on subsequent experiments 'save as' Sheet 2 or Sheet 3 or whatever. This enables you to modify the new 'saved as' sheet as much as you like without losing your original work.

When making changes, you're probably doing so to make the cash flow kinder, but remember, if you change something, to look for the knock-on effects. If you delay your sales drive, for example, you must also put back the income resulting from it.

When your cash flow changes give the best results possible, you may decide that including all your projects is too cash hungry. Go back to your project assessments form and look at it again with a view to eliminating some projects, starting with the ones giving least value for most expenditure. Try your cash flow forecast with each elimination, one by one, until you reach an acceptable picture.

! *Don't forget – if you cut out a project which might have increased sales, you must also adjust the sales line to take the lower sales into account.*

Your next step is to go back to the organisation chart and make sure that the remaining projects still make sense. If you are satisfied that this is the case, you can now finalise your project control form.

Profitability forecast

To check that you have achieved with your plan what you set out to do, a profit and loss forecast is necessary. So too is a forecast balance sheet, but you can probably find a short cut around that. In Appendix 6 you will find a profit forecast form. The computer model has all the formulae inserted already, so you don't have very much arithmetic to do.

The form looks a lot like the cash flow forecast, so why do you need to bother with it? The answer is that in the cash flow forecast you put in the income and expense when it actually occurs. In the P&L forecast you apportion the expenditure. For example, in motoring expenses you will have entered in the cash flow items for tax and insurance – probably in the same month, and possibly also service and MOT costs – making that month look terrible. However, bear in mind that this type of expense is not just for the month in which you incur it, but it may actually cover the whole year. It is what accountants call an *accrual*. In the P&L forecast you take the total expense for the item for the year, and divide it by 12. This gives a very different picture!

There are also some items in the P&L that you will not find in the cash flow. Depreciation is one major item – you know that assets for the most part reduce in value as they get older, so you need to be able to take account of that. Normally the taxman will allow you to write off motor vehicles at 25 per cent per year, computers at 33 per cent, and most other assets at 10 per cent. If you have any doubts about this, ask your accountant. We don't put it in the cash flow because you don't physically part with the cash, but it does need to be considered in your planning: hence this form.

When you've completed the form you'll be able to enter your new numbers on the ratio analysis form to check whether you've achieved what you intended to achieve with your plan. Purely balance sheet items like stock will not appear to have been altered, but if you normally hold a stock inventory of 5 per cent of your sales, then adjust the stock figure on your forecast to this as a closing level. Your project costs may have meant buying some equipment, and this less the depreciation on your entire asset pool should be added to your assets.

One thing you should do to check the reality of your plan is to look at what your resulting ratios will be. Do that by comparing your new figures with the ratio analysis form. Do the new figures look credible? Have they changed because of something you deliberately meant to do, or just because you have not taken all the factors into account?

When you have finally decided that this is the plan for you, you're ready to go on to the implementation stage.

The Business Plan

One of the best ways of making your business work better is to be absolutely clear about what you want it to achieve over the next few years – in other words, to have a plan. Appendix 4 and Appendix 4a are business plan documents. On the *Your business: make it work for you* disk you will find the same documents: they were created in Word 6 and there is also a .TXT (ASCII) version which you may be able to import into your own word processing package if you don't use Word 6. (For users of earlier systems a Word 2 version is also included.)

49

Somewhere in your aims and objectives section you will probably say that you intend to improve business performance by implementing your improvement plan. If you need help in creating your plan, look at Chapter 4 and rework the sections you aren't yet satisfied with. You may also find a trip to your local Business Link worth while here as it is sometimes difficult to be objective about your own business.

3

COMMON BUSINESS PROBLEMS

Avoid looking on this as the business equivalent of a medical dictionary – don't immediately worry if you do or don't actually have the symptoms you're reading about! This chapter is intended to serve more as a catalyst than as a diagnostic tool.

Business problems can perhaps be categorised in five different ways:

- start up
- expansion
- steady state
- contraction
- liquidation.

Start-up problems are outside the scope of this book.

EXPANSION

Most business people regard expansion as A Good Thing – and it may well be. If opportunities arise (or can be created) where expansion makes sense, all well and good. If to expand means that you have to 'buy sales', you could end up as a 'busy fool'.

The busy fool
The busy fool works progressively harder for the same or even less

money. Never forget that the real income for your business is gross margin (not percentage – *cash*).

If, as a result of chasing business, you end up with more work for lower gross margins, you are in danger of becoming a 'BF'. Look at the graph you produced on the ratio analysis form (Figure 3.1).

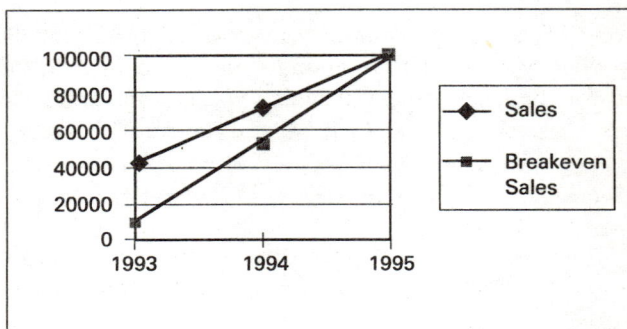

Figure 3.1 *The classic busy fool*

In Figure 3.1 the sales and break-even sales lines are converging, while both are increasing. This is quite common. The problem usually comes to a head either just before or just after the crossover point.

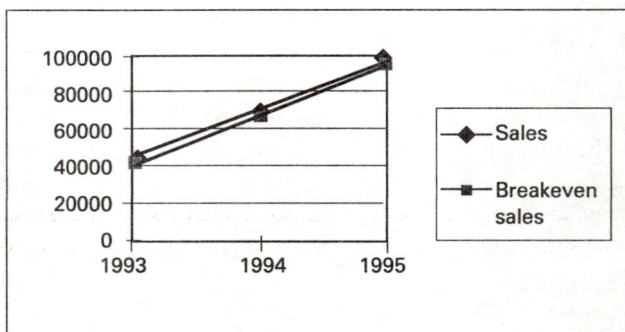

Figure 3.2 *The BF's best friend*

In Figure 3.2 the problem may be more difficult to spot. What happens, of course, is that the real income stays the same as the total business expands. Working capital increases with sales and this cannot be provided from income. Cash flow problems therefore ensue.

Over-trading

This is one of the most common causes of all business failures. It happens when you don't have enough money to finance the assets you need for the level of sales at which you are operating. You have the orders: on paper they can bring in good profit. But – and this is a big 'but' – you won't get paid for some time. You still have to pay the wages, you have to buy materials, and perhaps an extra piece of kit or two would make the whole thing more efficient. Sometimes you only take on the large commitment because of an existing debt problem and think that by working yourself to death you can save the business.

The outcome is predictable. You get late with payment so suppliers put you on stop. You go to the bank and your bank manager is unsympathetic: in many cases the bank has actually added to the problem by calling in your overdraft and other facilities because they can see you are getting deeper into difficulties. You fail to meet delivery dates because of your preoccupation with money problems, so your customers start to be difficult about paying you. You offer discounts or *anything* to get the money in. Cash flow worsens. The screw tightens. The business fails. That is over-trading.

Under-trading

Another major cause of business failure, under-trading, is often brought on by a general downturn in the economy, and sometimes because the market has now moved on and the management hasn't noticed.

As we have seen, the real income for a business is the gross margin (pounds not per cent – you can't spend percentages!) You can spend the margin on paying your overheads, preparing for the future and for having fun – you can also hoard it or waste it. In under-trading the gross margin progressively diminishes to the point where the margin is no longer able to pay overheads (ie less than break-even sales). Among the more common remedies for this type of problem are:

- cut overheads (often this will mean sales, advertising, market research and training);
- cut prices;
- call it a cash flow problem and borrow money to cover the short-fall;
- do nothing and wait for someone else to pull the plug.

The difficulty in dealing with this type of problem is not in deciding what action to take, but rather in diagnosing the *real* cause of the problem. Almost everyone I meet who has this problem blames the situation primarily on the economy; what they are really saying is, 'It is beyond me. I am helpless to do anything about it.'

If this is the situation you face, ask yourself which aspect of 'the economy' is causing your particular problem. How long has it been that way?

In many cases we can argue that the economy has changed little for several years. (Governments always tell us how much better things are, while businessmen and farmers say how much worse things are – and the day still has 24 hours.) Is it them or is it you?

Look again at the conditions in your market.

- Do the people who used to be your customers no longer exist?
- Are they there but have different needs?
- Are they there and buying from your direct competitors?
- Are they still there but no longer have any money to spend?

If you analyse these factors carefully, you will be in a position to develop a range of solutions. Let's take each of these scenarios in turn.

Loss of customers

If the people or businesses who used to buy from you no longer exist, you no longer have an adequate market. Apart from their disappearance, what do your absentee customers have in common? Are the factors geographic, demographic or economic? Have they 'gone away' or have they ceased to exist? What has happened to *their* market? Have they been replaced by similar business opportunities, or has the market died out?

A critical look here can save you a great deal of money, heartache and wasted effort. No matter how good you were at marketing, it is unlikely that you could breathe much life into the dodo grooming market, for instance!

If this may apply to your situation, look again at the market analysis form and stop flogging dead horses. If you are tempted to make a comment like '. . . it's all very well, but what can you expect in this business?' my answer would be to refer you first of all to a reliable source such as the Dun & Bradstreet International publication *Key Industrial Ratios*. Are you achieving the same results as the rest of your market? If not, the courses of action should begin to be apparent to you. If you are, and the business is really a poor performer, you need to ask whether this is going to be long term or will the market improve? A look at some historic evidence could be useful here. If you are in a market which is likely to perform poorly in the long term, perhaps you should consider getting out now. It takes luck and genius to turn round a market in this state, and you will be making your effort for the entire market, not just yourself: this could be expensive for you.

Consumer lifestyle changes

Your old customers are still around, but are satisfying their needs elsewhere. From whom and what are they buying? The landlords of a good many pubs have noticed a downturn in their trade. The customers are still around, but they are buying wine, beer and lager from a variety of non-pub sources to consume at home, rather than in the pub. In this case the market has changed apparently for the long term – drink/driving pressures, television, effective communications and education are all factors here. Carrying on as if nothing has happened means certain death for the pub business. What the publican can do about it comes down to these alternatives:

* competing for the social/entertainment aspect of the market need;
* competing for the physiological aspect of the market need;
* getting out while the going's good.

Successful strategies have resulted from all of these routes. Incidentally, 'getting out' doesn't necessarily mean selling up and leaving. It could well mean putting the buildings or grounds (facilities) to use in some other market.

Buying from your competitors

Your customers are still out there, but they are buying from your competitors. This should be the easiest situation to resolve (but not necessarily to win). Some industries face a battle they can't hope to win. The traditional baker, for example, is in competition with bread sales from supermarkets. Supermarkets – especially those with in-store bakeries – like bread sales. The smell of fresh bread does wonders for sales. Treating bread as a loss leader, many supermarkets cash in still further – 'if this smells so good and is so cheap, the rest of the store must be wonderful too' – like it or not, this approach seems to work! Supermarkets without in-store bakeries feel obliged to follow suit with their bread prices, so 'supermarket bread' is on the shelves daily at a price at which no one can make a profit. As a traditional baker, you won't be able to compete on price. A few bakers can compete because of geographical isolation, but probably not for much longer as supermarkets spread.

In this sort of situation, you will need to aim your business strategies at:

- competing on grounds other than price (this has been common in the past, but many supermarkets now have gained a reputation for quality products as good as if not better than most specialists);
- turning skills and equipment to use in a similar but not directly competing market (specialist products);
- campaigning for a level playing field;
- getting out of the business.

Once again, the longer the competition is allowed to take over your market, the more the new buying patterns become established, the more difficult it is for you to persuade your customers to come back to you, and the less money you have to fight the battle with. . . .

Different spending priorities

Your customers are there but they're choosing to spend their money on something else.

Given this situation, you will need to assess whether it is just a flash in the pan or symptomatic of some important factor in society today which means that your market is gone for ever.

A useful analogy here is the football pools business since the introduction of the National Lottery. Initially, football pools were seen very much as games of skill on which a moderate fortune could be won, while continuing the interest of the participant in the progress of his own team in the league. It could well be that this type of 'punter' was replaced almost totally by the numbers player, and that the football games lost all significance except as a device for deciding what the winning numbers should be.

In the meantime, demographic changes have weakened the ties between the 'punter' and football. When the National Lottery came along with its simplicity, ubiquity, high prizes and high profile, it seriously affected pools gambling. What can the pools companies do to retaliate?

First they need to recognise that their original customers are still in existence, and they are still buying the same product. It is hard to be certain what that product is, but it's probably something to do with a dream of happiness. They are buying that same product, but in different packaging. To survive, the pools businesses need to establish what it is the punters are buying. If your business is similarly threatened by new products, this is what you too need to establish. It may be that the market has sectors, some more easily won back than others.

The next stage is to establish whether this is a long-term situation or a short-term one. In the pools/lottery fight, it is interesting to see the number of different forces ranged against the National Lottery. Some are without doubt totally ideological, but all are capable of being utilised to lessen the impact, reduce the attraction and to shorten the life of the National Lottery. If it is not possible to achieve this within a reasonable space of time, the key to survival for the pools will have to be found by going back to their traditional 'skill and interest' base: the much smaller market catering for the football enthusiast.

MARGIN PROBLEMS

Gross margin is the difference between your sales and the direct cost to you of those sales. You spend the margin on your expenses and profits. What you do with that money will depend on the strategy you're following at the time, but the most important first step is to *break even*.

Every businessman should know what his break-even sales figure is. Many wish to know what the hourly figure is, others what the weekly figure is. The least anyone running a business should know is what the monthly figure is. One little spin-off from this is the way it can change how we look at the week. In retailing Saturday is the traditional end of the week. A bad Saturday means that you don't reach your targets because there's no time left in that week to recover. Using break-even monitoring and *starting* the week on Saturday means that you will have the whole of the week ahead in which to aim at recovery. Recouping a loss is far more difficult than just breaking even, and losses are cumulative.

Break-even is often expressed as an equivalent sales figure, and many in charge of businesses fool themselves by not understanding that if the gross margin is reduced, break-even sales are increased. Two useful formulae are:

Break-even sales = Expenses(overheads)/gross margin
Gross margin = Sales – Direct costs of sales.

Many businesses target their sales forces on order-taking targets which they confuse with sales. Sales are what goes out through the door, while order intake has to do with orders placed. The perennial problem in the medium to larger-sized business between 'sales' and 'production' can be solved, along with the profit margin worries, if the sales people are targeted primarily on gross margin. Any fool can give the product away and then complain because the works can't make it quickly enough. Earning the margin takes a real professional.

The rewards for taking this approach can be demonstrated clearly if you consider a business working on low margins. For instance, many couriers whose business is small work on 5 per cent gross margin. If such a business had a turnover of £100000, its gross margin would be £5000. If the sales price were increased by just 1 per cent, the new turnover (assuming no loss of sales) would be £101000. Reducing the cost of sales by 1 per cent at the same time would result in a saving of £950. The new gross margin would then be £6950. This represents an increase in real income of 39 per cent. Now that *is* worth doing the exercise for!

Another way of looking at this would be that to make the first income at the increased margin our courier would need only £72000 of sales, leaving him more time to do what he really wanted to do. Where gross margins are higher, the impact is less dramatic – but still worth the effort.

You may notice that throughout the discussion of the cases above, blaming the economy and resorting to the four most common remedies (cutting overheads, reducing prices, borrowing more money and doing nothing) have not been seen as appropriate.

The two main situations are where the margin is poor as a percentage, or where the percentage is good, but the profit yielded does not meet the income demand. The low margin percentage is a dangerous position to be in unless you have plenty of money in reserve. Take the courier example above with its 5 per cent margin:

Sales £100 000

Cost of sales £95 000

Gross margin £5000

It now experiences a swing of 1 per cent lost off selling price and at the same time incurs a 1 per cent increase in the cost of sales. This would give:

Sales (£100 000 – 1%)	= £99 000
Cost of sales (£95 000 +1%)	= £95 950
Gross margin	= £3050

As small changes like these have such a massive impact on profit, a minor disaster can wipe out a year's profit. If your business is in this position, your ability to survive rests on your reserves of capital.

If the situation appears unlikely to change for the foreseeable future – because of unavoidable market pressures – an exit strategy may be appropriate.

Where percentage margin is good, but does not provide an adequate income, solutions fall in either increasing volume with the same or similar products (products yielding good margins) or reducing overheads.

Shortage of cash

Many businesses suffer from shortage of cash, the possible causes for which may include:

1. Margin not good enough
2. Too much credit given
3. Bad debt
4. Taking too much out of the business yourself
5. Overheads too high
6. Non-cash asset base too large
7. Inappropriate financial control either internally or at the bank.

Businesses suffering from shortage of cash will either solve the problem or die. It is possible to stagger from crisis to crisis but, in the longer term, one or other of those two outcomes will happen.

However, before you reach the conclusion that death is the answer, look at the alternative routes first.

Margin not good enough

Go back and look again at the discussions we have already had about margin problems.

Too much credit given

From your ratio analysis sheet, you can see how much credit you give: it's called 'debtor days'.

Many of my clients tell me this figure is wrong, pointing out that they give 30 days' credit and none of their customers abuses this. However, further investigation often reveals that they invoice only at the end of each month. One client who provided teaching services to a school invoiced once a term, because the school paid out only once a term, normally about six weeks after the start of the next term. He believed he was giving 42 days' credit, and could not understand at all why his cash flow indicated a need for 133 days' funding. In reality, from the first unpaid day through to pay day, his debtor days were averaging 67 days (133 divided by 2 – the average between the oldest and most recent unpaid day) rather than the 42 days he imagined!

An interesting twist to the story occurred when he was involved in a department budget meeting and compared credit given by other suppliers (of equipment) and was told that they were all treated equally in that they were paid on the 12th day of the month after invoicing. When my client pointed out that his average supply date was six weeks older than that and he was thus unfairly treated, the school staff were shocked. They had not appreciated that this was the situation (this was how it had always been . . .) and immediately agreed to monthly invoicing. This was still not good, but it put £6000 into my client's pocket at a time when he needed it.

Look at your own ratio analysis form now. Line 39 shows your debtor days figure. Do the following calculation:

Let nominal debtor days = A

(if you give 30 days' credit A = 30

if you give 15 days' credit A = 15, and so on)

$$\frac{(\text{line } 39 - A) \times \text{line } 17}{\text{line } 39}$$

That is the extra sum of money you would have right now if your credit control was working well. (If the answer is zero your credit control is working well or you have no sales.)

Bad debt

During the recession bad debt was often blamed for business failure – one bad apple turning the whole barrel rotten. The truth is actually nearer to the fact that lots of sloppy credit management went on. You can't have a bad debt if you've already been paid!
Tips:

• Give credit only for valid reasons (see credit control in Chapter 1).
• Always put a 'pay by' date on your invoice, not just '30 days net'.

Taking too much out of the business yourself

This is not uncommon. Many good businesses have failed for this reason. If the owner of a good business has consistently and thoroughly emptied the till, when the hard times come he can either put money back or he cannot (because it has been spent). If he is unable to fund the business himself, he will normally turn to a lender. The picture the lender will see is one either of a profligate person, or of one who was smart enough to get his cash out while the going was good. Neither of these is a good prospect as a borrower!

Overheads too high

Overheads can eat cash. Features which do not show in your drawings may include the unnecessarily luxurious car or the hobby toys (computer, perhaps) etc. It may also be that you are paying for things you don't need, or have even forgotten about. Check your direct debit mandate statement at the bank. Go through your overheads in the accounts to be certain you are getting value for money.

Non-cash asset base too high

For the smaller business, distinguishing between the different sorts of asset is sometimes pointless. If shortage of cash is a problem, then remember our earlier definition of assets (that which the business needs to finance).

Realising (receiving cash for) assets need not mean selling the family silver – it could mean reducing stocks (holding consignment stocks instead), shortening the production cycle, reducing work in progress. All these activities either reduce your cash outlay or bring the cash in more quickly. Buying the freehold of your place of business is one of the easier ways of inducing a cash flow problem!

Inappropriate financial control

This can be caused by you or by the bank. It may be inflicted by the bank because its staff don't know or understand your business or because, despite warnings, you haven't taken appropriate action yourself.

If you have not left it too late, cash management measures along the lines spelt out in this book are more likely to solve your cash flow problem than any borrowing can.

Negotiation problems

A number of business people I meet are paying the wrong price for the goods or services they purchase. This will, of course, show up in low gross margin and poorer performance than the competition.

Many people, despite knowing this to be the case, don't like to raise the issue with their supplier, but look elsewhere for an alternative source. It is not always necessary. Your supplier would rather talk to you about the way he supplies you to see if real value can be added to the deal. In many cases you will both end up with a better deal than before.

Look once more at your analysis. Are you happy now that you have isolated the problems you want to address with your business improvement plan? If so, proceed to the next stage. If not, either go back through the process with a more critical eye, or ask for help. Your local Business Link, your accountant, your bank manager or even a friend may be able to help you by asking the simple question 'Why?' when you discuss what you are trying to achieve.

4

CREATING YOUR BUSINESS PLAN

On the disk you will find two plan format documents. They also
appear in the book as Appendix 4 and Appendix 4a. Use whichever
format you prefer. Some people find the style of the format in
Appendix 4a offers more scope for 'selling' the proposition, which
may be appropriate if you are in the market to attract funds for your
business. Both formats have their merits. The format in Appendix 4
is simpler to use for those who want to show themselves they have
solved their strategic problems. It is also familiar to many bank
managers.

METHOD OF PREPARATION

You have the analysis forms (Appendices 1–3), your project control
form on which you have identified your improvement projects, and
from Chapter 2 your cash flow and profitability forecasts. If this
isn't the case, you will need to go back and follow the steps in
Chapter 2 to get the best out of your business plan.

You can, of course, start from the title page, typing in your business name at the paragraph mark (use the 'show all marks' view on
your computer when you do this). However, what I prefer to do,
when using the Appendix 4a approach, is to start with the mecha-
nistic bits on page 1. Putting in name, address etc gets the 'paper'

dirty and the job under way. Next I do the introduction – a simple statement of why we have gone to all the trouble of preparing a business plan. I then skip straight to page 4 and spell out in detail there my objectives and strategy.

You will have a plan in outline in your rough analysis sheets and project control form. Your objectives are what you intend to achieve by making the planned changes. Your strategy is how you intend to put those changes into place.

If you decide to use the Appendix 4 plan, which has the advantage of being familiar to many bank managers, all of this section should be covered in the 'Business aims and objectives' section on page 1.

In Chapter 2 we covered how to complete the cash flow forecast, and you should have re-worked it to reflect your final intended plan. This will show if you need to raise funding. At this point the nature of the funding isn't critical – knowing how much you need, why you need it and what you mean to do with it is all you need now. Enter the information under 'Finance required' on page 90 (Appendix 4a).

It is no accident that the section on security comes next to the section on how much funding you need. Even if you don't intend to borrow from an 'institution' it is still worth listing the security (especially for sole traders and partners, just to remind yourself of what you stand to lose). The rest of the plan is about the history and feel of the business. You might ask 'if I'm not borrowing any money, why do I need to do all this?' One simple answer is because it makes you think even harder about your business and how to get it working for you.

In order to complete the rest of the plan, you are going to conduct or report a SWOT analysis (SWOT stands for Strengths, Weaknesses, Opportunities, Threats).

Most of us have been brought up not to blow our own trumpet, and many people have trouble identifying their strengths and weaknesses. I usually start the process with clients by asking, 'Where do you see the bulk of your opportunities coming from?' Write down your answer to that question, and go on to, 'What are the main threats that your business faces in the next year or so?' (Threats often come from competition, the economy, owner's health, legislation, and so on. . . .)

Then consider the question, 'Where do you feel the business is least able to take advantage of the opportunities (and/or defend itself from the threats)?' followed by, 'What are the business's best aspects in taking advantage of the opportunities and/or defending itself against the threats?'

Relating the issues to the business rather than to the owner takes away much of the subjectivity of the potential responses to SWOT questions.

When you have entered these details and appended your project control plan, cash flow and profitability forecasts, you can say that you have a good quality business plan. So now all you have to do is to put it all in the bottom drawer of your desk and everything in it will happen as planned . . . won't it? Well, no, it won't! You now need to hammer out some implementation procedures.

IMPLEMENTING THE PLAN

Most people in business have some document that they work to – probably a diary, calendar or wall planner. Whatever you use, that's where to enter your planned actions.

Your business plan includes changes to your business. Some of those changes will happen as a result of things you intend to do; but they aren't the ones I want you to record. What I want you to set out in your diary are the *planned* actions.

In Appendix 7 you have set out your major projects, with their time scales. You now need to break the projects down into individual bite-size chunks. If you set out each little step you intend to complete each week, you stand a strong chance of getting the job done. If you leave the projects in 'global' terms, such as 'to be completed in six months' time', you (like me and practically everyone else!) will put it off until next week, next month . . . it won't get done, will it?

Your weekly ration of improvement project will ensure:

- steady progress
- enough resources to run the business at the same time.

That's it. You now have everything you need to make your business work for you. I wish you the best of luck with your endeavours.

Many of the ideas discussed in this book will be available for discussion at your local Business Link.

If you experience any difficulty implementing activities suggested in this book, do ask for help from any of the professional sources mentioned. Your local Business Link is a good place to start if you're not sure where to seek help.

Appendix 1

RATIO ANALYSIS FORM

	A	B	C	D	E	F
1	**Data collection**					
2						
3	Year	1st	2nd	3rd	4th	Ind ave
4	Items	£	£	£	£	£
5	Current assets					
6	Current liabilities					
7	Sales					
8	Working capital	0	0	0	0	
9	Total debt					
10	Net worth					
11	Earnings before int/tax	0	0	0	0	
12	Net profit					
13	Debtors					
14	Cost of goods sold					
15	Average stock					
16	Fixed assets					
17	Total assets	0	0	0	0	
18	Gross profit	#VALUE!	#VALUE!	#VALUE!	#VALUE!	
19	Expenses/overheads	#VALUE!	#VALUE!	#VALUE!	#VALUE!	
20	Net interest charged					
21	Total operating expenses					
22	Other operating income					
23	Trade creditors					
24	Preferential creditors					
25						
26	**Key operating ratios**					
27						
28	Current assets/current liabilities	#DIV/0!	#DIV/0!	#DIV/0!	#DIV/0!	
29	Sales/working capital	#VALUE!	#VALUE!	#VALUE!	#VALUE!	
30	Total debt/net worth	#DIV/0!	#DIV/0!	#DIV/0!	#DIV/0!	
31	EBIT/ sales	#VALUE!	#VALUE!	#VALUE!	#VALUE!	
32	Net profit/sales	#VALUE!	#VALUE!	#VALUE!	#VALUE!	

	A	B	C	D	E	F
33	Net profit/net worth	#DIV/0!	#DIV/0!	#DIV/0!	#DIV/0!	
34	Net profit/total assets	#DIV/0!	#DIV/0!	#DIV/0!	#DIV/0!	
35	Debtors x 365/sales	#VALUE!	#VALUE!	#VALUE!	#VALUE!	
36	Cost of goods sold/average stock	#VALUE!	#VALUE!	#VALUE!	#VALUE!	
37	Fixed assets/net worth	#DIV/0!	#DIV/0!	#DIV/0!	#DIV/0!	
38	Sales/total assets	#VALUE!	#VALUE!	#VALUE!	#VALUE!	
39	Gross profit/sales	#VALUE!	#VALUE!	#VALUE!	#VALUE!	
40						
41	**Break-even calculations**					
42						
43	Break-even sales	#VALUE!	#VALUE!	#VALUE!	#VALUE!	
44	Break-even gap	#VALUE!	#VALUE!	#VALUE!	#VALUE!	
45	Quick profit	#VALUE!	#VALUE!	#VALUE!	#VALUE!	
46	Quick profit/sales	#VALUE!	#VALUE!	#VALUE!	#VALUE!	
47	Net profit before tax Value (£000s)	#VALUE!	#VALUE!	#VALUE!	#VALUE!	
48	% of sales	#VALUE!	#VALUE!	#VALUE!	#VALUE!	
49						
50	**Funding need calculation**					
51						
52	Sales	0	0	0	0	
53	Stock Value (£000s)	0	0	0	0	
54	Stock % of sales	#VALUE!	#VALUE!	#VALUE!	#VALUE!	
55	Debtors Value (£000s)	0	0	0	0	
56	Debtors % of sales	#VALUE!	#VALUE!	#VALUE!	#VALUE!	
57	Trade creditors Value (£000s)	0	0	0	0	
58	Trade creditors % of sales	#VALUE!	#VALUE!	#VALUE!	#VALUE!	
59	Preferential creditors Value (£000s)	0	0	0	0	
60	Preferential creditors % of sales	#VALUE!	#VALUE!	#VALUE!	#VALUE!	
61	Net working assets Value (£000s)	0	0	0	0	
62	Net working assets % of sales	#VALUE!	#VALUE!	#VALUE!	#VALUE!	
63	Creditor strain					
64	Trade credit strain Value (£000s)	#VALUE!	#VALUE!	#VALUE!	#VALUE!	
65	% of sales	#VALUE!	#VALUE!	#VALUE!	#VALUE!	
66	Preferential cred str. Value (£000s)	#VALUE!	#VALUE!	#VALUE!	#VALUE!	
67	% of sales	#VALUE!	#VALUE!	#VALUE!	#VALUE!	
68	True net working assets					
69	Value (£000s)	#VALUE!	#VALUE!	#VALUE!	#VALUE!	
70	% of sales	#VALUE!	#VALUE!	#VALUE!	#VALUE!	
71						
72						
73						
74						
75						
76						
77						
78	**Banker's ratios**					
79						
80	Profit sensitivity	#VALUE!	#VALUE!	#VALUE!	#VALUE!	
81	Capital gearing	#DIV/0!	#DIV/0!	#DIV/0!	#DIV/0!	
82	Interest cover	#DIV/0!	#DIV/0!	#DIV/0!	#DIV/0!	

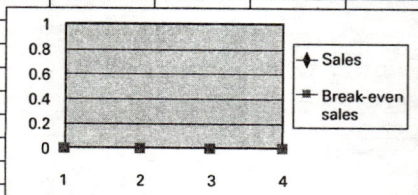

Chart legend: Sales, Break-even sales

Appendix 2

MARKET ANALYSIS FORM

Products \ Customers	Same customers	More of the same type of customer	Totally different types of customer
Same products or services			
Modified or extra similar products or services			
Products or services totally new to you			

Appendix 3

ORGANISATION ANALYSIS FORM

	Existing	Extension of existing	Modified	Entirely new	Project start and end dates	Project cost
Marketing Products/services Markets Customers Geographical areas Channels Competition Sales organisation Distributors Suppliers Promotional mix						
Resources needed Premises and access Equipment Labour Materials Transport/distribution Selling Stock						
Management *Organisation of:* • Production • Markets • Finance • Technical *Systems for:* • Finance • Other information • Quality						

Appendix 4

BUSINESS PLAN

Business name

_____

Owner's name

_____

Position in the firm

_____

Business address

_____

Business aims and objectives

Capital required to start the business

Capital available

Extra capital needed to start

Capital reserve

Other sources of finance

Owner's essential personal drawings

Fixed assets to be purchased

Minimum stock/materials costs for starting the business

Important contacts and people

Business advisor

Bank manager

Accountant

Solicitor

Key staff (at start of business)

Key staff (for future development)

Suppliers

Marketing strategy

Product/services to be offered

Future developments

Pricing policy and terms of trading

Principal competitors' prices and terms

Market average price and terms

Product(s)/services

Features   **Benefits**

Firm's own

Strengths   **Weaknesses**

Firm's own competitive edge

Target customers/consumers

Principal target groups and approximate size

Secondary target groups and approximate size

Possible future target groups

Market research programme

Principal competitors

    Name

    Address

    Strengths   **Weaknesses**

    Name

    Address

    Strengths   **Weaknesses**

How many customers are required to satisfy sales turnover?

How many potential customers need to be contacted?

Advertising programme

Sales promotion activity

Legal matters

Insurances

Other matters

Training requirements (proprietors and/or directors)

Immediate

Long term

Training requirements (employees)

Immediate

Long term

Contingency plans

What if . . . ?

Proposed action

What if . . . ?

Proposed action

What if . . . ?

Proposed action

What if . . . ?

Proposed action

Appendix 4a

BUSINESS PLAN

(ALTERNATIVE FORM)

Business name

Owner's name

Position in the firm

Business address

Introduction
Why the business plan was prepared
Index of pages

The business
When established, results to date, borrowing history, existing commitments, current bankers

Management
Key personnel, their experience, knowledge of the industry, age, education and training

Premises
Location, size, planning consent, health/safety, fire regulations, cost

Product(s)/services
Details of products or services offered, state of product
development, any follow-up products or services

Markets
Details of market, size, customers, competitors, basis of sales
estimates, and advertising methods, evidence of market
research

Objectives and strategy
Business objectives, timetable and assumptions, risk factors, long-term plans

Financial projections
See attached
To include projections of at least one year's future trading figures, with cash flow, profitability and projected balance sheet

Finance required
Total funding required based on projections, applications of those fundings, repayment assumptions; purpose of finance, detailing capital expenditure

Security available
Assets available as security (personal as well as business), and also assets used as security elsewhere

Management information systems
Accounting and other systems used by the business, including ability to produce regular management accounts

Principal risks
Most likely areas of risk and ability to cope with these, including what happens in the event of injury to or sickness of key personnel

Appendix 5

CASH FLOW FORECAST

Name of business						
Forecast for period starting						
Orders taken						
Dated	**Month**	**Pre-start**	**1**	**2**	**3**	**4**
Receipts						
Cash sales						
Credit sales						
Other income (Grant)						
Capital introduced						
Loans received						
VAT reclaimed						
A Total receipts		0	0	0	0	0
Payments						
Cash purchases						
Payments to creditors						
Employee wages & NI						
Own drawings/NI						
Motoring costs						
Rent & rates						
Postage & packaging						
Advertising & printing						
Heat, light & power						
Telephone						
Professional fees						
Insurance						
Repairs & renewals						
Bank charges & interest						
Sundry expenses						
Loan repayment (bank)						
Loan repayment (other)						
VAT payments						
Capital purchases						
B Total payments	0	0	0	0	0	0
C Cash flow surplus (deficit) A–B	0	0	0	0	0	0
Opening bank balance	0	0	0	0	0	0
Closing bank balance	0	0	0	0	0	0

5	6	7	8	9	10	11	12	Total
								0
								0
								0
								0
								0
								0
								0
0	0	0	0	0	0	0	0	0
								0
								0
								0
								0
								0
								0
								0
								0
								0
								0
								0
								0
								0
								0
								0
								0
								0
								0
								0
								0
0	0	0	0	0	0	0	0	0
0	0	0	0	0	0	0	0	0
0	0	0	0	0	0	0	0	0
0	0	0	0	0	0	0	0	0

Appendix 6

PROFITABILITY FORECAST

Name of business					
Period starting					
Income	Month 1	Month 2	Month 3	Month 4	Month 5
Sales					
Other generated					
Total income	0	0	0	0	0
Direct costs					
Materials					
Consumables					
Labour					
Total direct costs	0	0	0	0	0
Gross profit	0	0	0	0	0
Expenditure					
Employees' wages					
Business premises					
Power/heat					
Repairs & maintenance					
Insurances					
Travel/motoring					
Telephone & postage					
Delivery & carriage					
Printing & stationery					
Advertising					
Marketing/promotion					
Accounts/legal fees					
Training & development					
Bank charges					
Bank interest					
Depreciation					
General expenditure					
Other					
Total expenditure	0	0	0	0	0
Net profit/(loss)	0	0	0	0	0
Cumulative profit/(loss)	0	0	0	0	0
Drawings					

Month 6	Month 7	Month 8	Month 9	Month 10	Month 11	Month 12	Totals
							0
							0
							0
							0
0	0	0	0	0	0	0	0
							0
							0
							0
0	0	0	0	0	0	0	0
0	0	0	0	0	0	0	0
							0
							0
							0
							0
							0
							0
							0
							0
							0
							0
							0
							0
							0
							0
							0
							0
							0
							0
							0
0	0	0	0	0	0	0	0
0	0	0	0	0	0	0	0
0	0	0	0	0	0	0	0

Appendix 7

PROJECT CONTROL FORM

No.	Project	Month 1	Month 2	Month 3

Month 4	Month 5	Month 6	Month 7	Month 8	Month 9	Month 10	Month 11	Month 12

Appendix 8

RATIO ANALYSIS FORM

	A	B
1	**Data collection**	
2		
3	Year	1st
4	Items	£
5	Current assets	
6	Current liabilities	
7	Sales	
8	Working capital	=SUM(B5–B6)
9	Total debt	.
10	Net worth	
11	Earning before interest/tax	=SUM(B12+B20)
12	Net profit	
13	Debtors	
14	Cost of goods sold	
15	Average stock	
16	Fixed assets	
17	Total assets	=SUM(B5+B16)
18	Gross profit	=SUM(B7–B14)
19	Expenses/overheads	=SUM(B21–B20)
20	Net interest charged	
21	Total operating expenses	
22	Other operating income	
23	Trade creditors	
24	Preferential creditors	
25	**Key operating ratios**	
26		
27	Current assets/current liabilities	=SUM(B5/B6)
28	Sales/working capital	=SUM(B7/B8)
29	Total debt/net worth	=SUM(B13/B14)
30	EBIT/sales	=SUM(B15/B11)
31	Net profit/sales	=SUM(B16/B11)
32	Net profit/net worth	=SUM(B16/B14)
33	Net profit/total assets	=SUM(B16/B21)

APPENDIX 8: RATIO ANALYSIS FORM

	A	B
34	Debtors x 365/sales	=SUM(B17*365/B11)
35	Cost of goods sold/average stock	=SUM(B18/B19)
36	Fixed assets/net worth	=SUM(B20/B14)
37	Sales/total assets	=SUM(B11/B21)
38	Gross profit/sales	=SUM(B22/B11)
39		
40	**Break-even calculations**	
41		
42	Break-even sales	=SUM(B25/B43
43	Break-even gap	=SUM(B11–B47)
44	Quick profit	=SUM(B48*B43)
45	Quick profit/sales	=SUM(B49/B11)
46	Net profit before tax Value(£000s)	=SUM(B49+B26)
47	% of sales	=SUM(B51/B11)
48		
49	**Funding need calculation**	
50		
51	Sales	=SUM(B11)
52	Stock Value (£000s)	=SUM(B19)
53	Stock % of sales	=SUM(B57/B11)
54	Debtors Value (£000s)	=SUM(B17)
55	Debtors % of sales	=SUM(B59/B11)
56	Trade creditors Value (£000s)	=SUM(B27)
57	Trade creditors % of sales	=SUM(B61/B11)
58	Preferential creditors Value (£000s)	=SUM(B28)
59	Preferential creditors % of sales	=SUM(B63/B11)
60	Net working assets Value (£000s)	=SUM(B57+B59-B61–B63)
61	Net working assets % of sales	=SUM(B65/B11)
62	Creditor strain	
63	Trade credit strain Value (£000s)	=SUM(B69*B11)
64	% of sales	=IF(((B62–0.1)<=(0)),0,(B62–0.1))
65	Preferential cred str. Value (£000s)	=SUM(B71*B11)
66	% of sales	=IF(((B64–0.05)<=(0)),0,(B64–0.05))
67	True net working assets	
68	Value (£000s)	=SUM(B65+B68+B70)
69	% of sales	=SUM(B73/B11)
70		
71	**Banker's ratio**	
72		
73	Profit sensitivity	=SUM(B48)/B11
74	Capital gearing	=SUM(B13)/B14
75	Interest cover	=SUM(B15)/B24

97

Appendix 9

WORKED EXAMPLE: TRANSFERRING DATA FROM ACCOUNTS TO ANALYSIS FORM

Here is a set of accounts for a fictitious business. The accounts contain the most common complications so that we can see how to deal with them. If you don't have such complexities in your accounts, don't worry – just feed in the figures you have. If for some reason some of your figures are not available, that doesn't matter: the rest of the program will work for you, and it will give you a strong pointer to the questions you need to be asking your accountant.

The worked example contains the three key pages from the annual accounts:

1. The balance sheet
2. The profit and loss account
3. Notes on the accounts.

Your published accounts, or those you send to the Inland Revenue, may well be in this form and the notes to the accounts show the detail of what your accountant has done.

Working from the ratio analysis sheet, and starting at the top, you will see current assets. Line 9 of the balance sheet is the figure you need. Be careful to enter it under the correct year. One of the unfortunate conventions is that the most recent year in accounts is on the left side of the page, but your ratio analysis form is laid out in the conventional way to give you a graph with the most recent year on the right, so take care not to get in a muddle here.

Current liabilities is next, but you may have a little difficulty finding these, as accountants sometimes use the term 'amounts falling due within one year'. This is the case here and you could enter £204221 in the analysis form at line 10. I recommend that at this point you look at the notes to the accounts. In the creditors section is an item called 'directors' loan account'. The directors of this business have put their money into the business as a loan, so that in due course they can take it back out again without paying tax on it.

Whether or not this is a sensible thing to do depends on circumstances. In reality, they would not think of taking the money out unless the business could afford it. Here, as you can see, the business has far greater current debts than assets and should notify Companies House that it is trading insolvently.

It is not the purpose of this section to go into insolvency rules, but if you have accounts that show this sort of feature you may wish to remove the directors' loan account from the current assets to the long-term debt by signing an undertaking to the effect that the loan is not for repayment in the current financial year. In this case you could use the figure from the balance sheet (BS) or deduct from it the £103519 of directors' loan. Since it is nearer the real truth, I would deduct the loan from the current account, leaving £100702 in line 10 of the ratio analysis form (RAF).

Sales – sometimes called turnover – can be found in the profit and loss account (P&L), which is the very first figure in the account. Enter this at line 1.

If you are working on the computerised model of the RAF, working capital will now have appeared on your form. If you are working manually, you arrive at this figure by deducting line 10 from line 9.

Total debt is a little calculation you will need to do for yourself. I have not built it into the form because most British companies I deal with these days do not have long-term finance! All you need to do is add together current liabilities from line 10 plus the amounts falling due after one year. This you enter in line 13. In the case mentioned above, one needs to remember to add back in the directors' loan account figure.

Earnings before interest and tax can be seen easily in the P&L in this case, but it is called the 'operating profit'. Some accounts don't

show this and it is obtained easily from other sources. To get this figure from accounts which don't specify it, you take the net profit and
add to it the interest paid plus any business tax paid. If you are a sole
trader or partnership, don't include income tax here as that is your
personal tax, not the tax of the business.

Net profit is found at the bottom of the P&L and should be
entered at line 16. Debtors in line 17 are lurking in the current assets
section of the balance sheet. Normally the reason for looking at
debtors is to give you a measure of how good you are at getting paid
(or how bad your customers are at paying you). If you look at the
notes to the accounts, you will find that in this case there are two
items in the debtors section: trade debtors and prepayments.
Prepayments are the result of your arrangements with your suppliers
(most often the landlord whom you may pay perhaps up to six
months in advance). If your year end came one month after you had
paid six months in advance your accounts would show a prepayment
of five months' rent. This has nothing to do with how you get paid,
so enter the figure for trade debtors only in line 17.

The cost of goods sold should be entered in line 18. This does not
normally present a problem, but if you manufacture or modify the
goods before you sell them – as is the case with this company – the
question of what to do with productive labour arises. As a guide, it
would be sensible (provided you have the information available)
always to add the cost of productive labour to the materials costs to
arrive at the cost of goods sold. However, this is not always possible.
Some businesses only have one or two figures for labour costs, *wages
for the employees* and *drawings for the owners*. If there is some logic in
your accounts, such as that all your labour or a clearly defined amount
of it is productive (sometimes called direct), use that figure in the cost
of goods sold. If you are a one-man band don't put your drawings or
any part of them as labour: to do so would be unacceptable to the
Inland Revenue.

Where it is difficult to separate the direct from the indirect, it
would be sensible to put it into cost of goods sold if that is where
most of it would naturally fall. If this is not the case, include it as
overheads. One little check you can make to simplify the issue is to
look at the variation month on month of your wages bill. If your sales
go up and down but the wages bill stays more or less constant, there
is a strong argument for putting wages in overheads. If they vary
directly or considerably with sales, there is an equally strong argument
for putting them in cost of goods sold.

Whichever way you decide, make sure that your treatment of this item is consistent throughout the study. If you changed accountants in the period you are studying, you will need to be particularly careful on this one. Different accountants will favour different practices on this issue and that is why so much explanation has been necessary. Whichever approach you choose, stick to it throughout.

Average stock in line 19 is obtained by taking the previous year's close, adding this year's close and dividing by two. I believe that, if you can put up with a slight inconsistency of having your stock figure six months out of phase, you can just use the closing stock figure for each year, entering them exactly as they are in line 19.

Fixed assets are normally straightforward, but in this case the directors have seen fit to include an investment in the assets of the business. The reasons for the inclusion are important. If the investment is to do with the real business such as buying a stake in your main customer to make sure you remain his major supplier, then that investment should be included in this analysis.

In this case the full notes to the accounts (which I have not published) show that the investment was one where the directors wanted to pay for it with untaxed money rather than take the money out of the business and then buy the asset. As it is only a tax convenience, I would be inclined to reduce the fixed assets by £5000 in 1993 and by £4950 in 1994. The total borrowing – particularly the directors' account – should be reduced by the same amount. This is not a moral judgement, but merely an attempt to rid the account of matters which can hide or blur the true business performance.

If you are using the computer version, lines 21 and 22 will be worked out for you. If not, you can obtain line 21 by adding line 9 to line 20; you will get line 22 by deducting line 18 from line 11.

Those working manually can find line 23 from the P&L account. A little care is needed here, as often the figures are represented in a different format with overhead, including interest, as one figure in the accounts. If you're using the computer version, all you need to do is put in the total overhead figure in line 25, with the interest paid in line 24. The program will work out for you the figure for line 23. In this case it is easier to put in the figures as for 1994 – £84 098 in line 23, £17 948, the net interest (£17 969–£21) as line 24; then add the two together to give line 25. Although the formula has been entered in your spreadsheet, you can easily override it by entering a number over the top.

Other trading (operating) income could arise from such things as grants, but will always, if appropriate, be identified in the accounts. If any are mentioned, enter in line 26. Normally if there is nothing to enter here I put a zero to remind me that I identified a zero figure rather than forgot to put the figure in.

It is usually necessary to look at the notes to the accounts for the trade creditors figure. Depending on circumstances, you may wish also to add in accruals. Accruals are the reverse of prepayments. If you pay your rent three months in arrears and your year end for accounts came one month before rent day, you would have an accrual of two months' rent (technically owed but not yet due for payment). If this is the case don't include it in the trade creditors figure. If it is an accrual which is due but hasn't been paid because your landlord forgot to send you the invoice, I would be inclined to include that which is in excess of the normal trading terms. This is not 'accountancy': it is simply that the main reason for looking at your trade creditors is to see what money you would have to find if your creditors pressed for payment in accordance with their terms and conditions.

Preferential creditors in accountancy terms are those creditors with a special claim on your assets. The law spells out which these are. For this purpose, a more liberal line is recommended. In the example, if you look at the notes to the accounts you will see seven listings under creditors. The ones I would include under preferential creditors are: bank overdraft, Social Security and other taxes. I would also ask about the nature of the loan account. It may be that it is legally binding to be paid by a certain time; it may equally apply that the loan shark from whom you borrowed the money will come and break both your legs if you don't pay on time. I would regard those as preferential creditors. If the reason for the inclusion in the current section is that you have no firm agreement to delay payment (a loan from the family often fits this bill where you pay it back when you can), then I would not include it in my list of preferential creditors. Whatever your decision, enter it at line 28.

Those who are using the computer-based version will now find that your report is complete and all the ratios have been worked out for you. If you're using the manual approach, check Appendix 8 for the formulae.

SAMPLE BALANCE SHEET

		1994		1993	**Enter on analysis sheet at line no.**
Fixed assets					
Tangible assets		195753		241052	*
Investments		4950		.5000	*
		200703		246052	20
Current assets					
Stocks	8273		9887		19
Debtors	28701		42325		17
Cash at bank	12		1119		
	36986		53331		9
Creditors					
Amounts due within one year	204221		217607		*
Net current assets		−167235		−164276	
Total assets less current liabilities		33468		81776	
Creditors Amounts falling due after more than one year		30135		66390	*
Net worth		3333		15386	14

* see note

103

SAMPLE TRADING PROFIT AND LOSS ACCOUNT

		1994	1993	Enter on analysis sheet at line no.
Turnover		184073	194542	11
Cost of sales		94133	90205	18
Gross profit		89940	104337	formula
Distribution costs and selling expenses	16566		14375	
Administative expenses	67532		63234	
		84098	77609	23
		5842	26728	
Other operating income		53	629	
Operating profit		5895	27357	15
Interest receivable		21	49	
		5916	27406	
Interest payable		17969	17958	24
Net profit		−12053	9448	16

NOTES ON THE ACCOUNTS

Debtors	1994	1993	Enter on analysis sheet at line no.
Trade debtors	25436	34849	17
Prepayments	3265	7476	
	28701	42325	

Creditors
Amounts falling due within one year

Bank overdraft	5085	18133	*
Directors' loan account	103519	0	*
Loan account	1904	93658	*
Hire purchase	63324	79347	*
Trade creditors	9989	13218	27
Accruals	2469	4517	*
Social Security and other taxes	17881	8734	*
	204171	217607	

Amounts falling due after more than one year

Hire purchase	30135	66390	*

Share capital

Allotted and fully paid up	40000	40000	*

* see note

RATIO ANALYSIS FORM: THE WORKED EXAMPLE

	A	B	C	D	E	F	G
1							
2							
3							
4							
5	Data collection						
6							
7	Year	1st	2nd	1993	1994	Ind ave	
8	Items	£	£	£	£	£	
9	Current assets			53331	36986		
10	Current liabilities			217607	100702		
11	Sales			194542	184073		
12	Working capital	0	0	−164276	−63716		
13	Total debt			283997	234356		
14	Net worth			15386	3333		
15	Earnings before int/tax	0	0	27357	5895		
16	Net profit			9448	−12053		
17	Debtors			34849	25436		
18	Cost of goods sold			90205	94133		
19	Average stock			9887	8273		
20	Fixed assets			241052	195753		
21	Total assets	0	0	294383	232739		
22	Gross profit	#VALUE!	#VALUE!	104337	89940		
23	Expenses/overheads	#VALUE!	#VALUE!	59700	66150		
24	Net interest charged			17909	17948		
25	Total operating expenses			77609	84098		
26	Other operating income			629	53		
27	Trade creditors			13218	9989		
28	Preferential creditors			120525	24870		
29							
30	Key operating ratios						
31							
32	Current assets/current liabilities	#DIV/0!	#DIV/0!	0.24508	0.367282		
33	Sales/working capital	#VALUE!	#VALUE!	−1.18424	−2.88896		
34	Total debt/net worth	#DIV/0!	#DIV/0!	18.4581	70.31383		
35	EBIT/ sales	#VALUE!	#VALUE!	0.14062	0.032025		
36	Net profit/sales	#VALUE!	#VALUE!	0.04857	−0.06548		
37	Net profit/net worth	#DIV/0!	#DIV/0!	0.61406	−3.61626		
38	Net profit/total assets	#DIV/0!	#DIV/0!	0.03209	−0.05179		
39	Debtors x 365/sales	#VALUE!	#VALUE!	65.3837	50.43727		
40	Cost of goods sold/average stock	#VALUE!	#VALUE!	9.1236	11.37834		
41	Fixed assets/net worth	#DIV/0!	#DIV/0!	15.667	58.73177		
42	Sales/total assets	#VALUE!	#VALUE!	0.66085	0.790899		
43	Gross profit/sales	#VALUE!	#VALUE!	0.53632	0.48861		
44							
45	Break-even calculations						
46							
47	Break-even sales	#VALUE!	#VALUE!	144706	172116.6		
48	Break-even gap	#VALUE!	#VALUE!	49835.8	11956.35		
49	Quick profit	#VALUE!	#VALUE!	26728	5842		
50	Quick profit/sales	#VALUE!	#VALUE!	0.13739	0.031737		

	A	B	C	D	E	F	G
51	Net profit before tax Value (£000s)	#VALUE!	#VALUE!	27357	5895		
52	% of sales	#VALUE!	#VALUE!	0.14062	0.032025		
53							
54	**Funding need calculations**						
55							
56	Sales	0	0	194542	184073		
57	Stock Value (£000s)	0	0	9887	8273		
58	Stock % of sales	#VALUE!	#VALUE!	0.05082	0.044944		
59	Debtors Value (£000s)	0	0	34849	25436		
60	Debtors % of sales	#VALUE!	#VALUE!	0.17913	0.138184		
61	Trade creditors Value (£000s)	0	0	13218	9989		
62	Trade creditors % of sales	#VALUE!	#VALUE!	0.06794	0.054267		
63	Preferential creditors Value (£000s)	0	0	120525	24870		
64	Preferential creditors % of sales	#VALUE!	#VALUE!	0.61953	0.135109		
65	Net working assets Value (£000s)	0	0	-89007	-1150		
66	Net working assets % of sales	#VALUE!	#VALUE!	0.45752	-0.00625		
67	Creditor strain						
68	Trade credit strain Value (£000s)	#VALUE!	#VALUE!	0	0		
69	% of sales	#VALUE!	#VALUE!	0	0		
70	Preferential cred str. Value (£000s)	#VALUE!	#VALUE!	110798	15666.35		
71	% of sales	#VALUE!	#VALUE!	0.56953	0.085109		
72	True net working assets						
73	Value (£000s)	#VALUE!	#VALUE!	21790.9	14516.35		
74	% of sales	#VALUE!	#VALUE!	0.11201	0.078862		
75							
76							
77							
78							
79							
80							
81							
82	**Banker's ratios**						
83							
84	Profit sensitivity	#VALUE!	#VALUE!	0.25617	0.064954		
85	Capital gearing	#DIV/0!	#DIV/0!	18.4581	70.31383		
86	Interest cover	#DIV/0!	#DIV/0!	1.52756	0.328449		

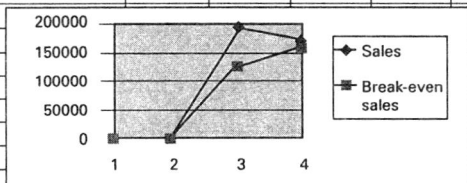

Chart (rows 75–82): Line graph with y-axis values 0, 50000, 100000, 150000, 200000 and x-axis values 1, 2, 3, 4. Legend: Sales, Break-even sales.

Appendix 10

PROJECT ASSESSMENT FORM

No.	Problem area	Project	Priority

Cost	Payback value	Start date	Finish date

INDEX